Civic Self-respect

Civic Self-respect

RALPH NADER

Seven Stories Press
New York · Oakland · London

Seven Stories Press
140 Watts Street
New York, NY 10013
www.sevenstories.com

Library of Congress Cataloging-in-Publication Data is on file.

ISBN: 978-1-64421-278-3 (paperback)
ISBN: 978-1-64421-279-0 (ebook)

College professors and high school and middle school teachers may order free examination copies of Seven Stories Press titles. Visit https://www.sevenstories.com/pg/resources-academics or email academic@sevenstories.com.

Printed in the United States of America

9 8 7 6 5 4 3 2 1

Contents

Preface vii

1. I, the Citizen 1

2. I, the Worker 27

3. I, the Consumer-Shopper 41

4. I, the Taxpayer 57

5. I, the Voter 71

6. I, the Parent 83

7. I, the Veteran 99

8. I, the Philanthropist 115

9. Conclusion 135

10. Appendix 139

Resources for Action 141

How to Read This Book to Maximize Motivation

There is nothing better in civic awareness than person-to-person contact. Keep that in mind as you read this short book—and if possible do it with a like-minded friend, family member, or colleague.

Civic action strengthens democracy's production of justice, opportunity, and the good life for all, and this isn't the first book to be written about it. Alas, like consumer-protection guides that tell the reader to fight back, these types of books are too little used. Even the bestsellers are rarely put to use. Why? I think it is because the gap between where the reader is and where the author wants the reader to go is too wide. This book strives to start with ordinary people, like you and me, who show signs of wanting to elevate their daily lives for more meaning, better living standards, and less aggravating surrenders to oppressive powers. Here are the stages of entry:

Stage One is simply doing your part to upgrade your game. You become a smarter consumer, voter, worker, and so forth in registering your wishes, complaints, and choices.

Stage Two is connecting with organizations about what you would like to see done, joining their ranks, and pursuing their just causes.

Stage Three is pioneering a mission that, to your knowledge, no one in your community, state, country, or the world has pursued, when you start a new drive, movement, or civic group. This latter stage is not as pie-in-the-sky as it may appear. After all, the millions of individual and civic associations fighting for justice and fair play were each started by someone at this stage. The idea behind the three-stage approach is to bring to bear your own situation, temperament, and skill—or to make use of the cool indignation you might feel after an awful experience that you want to prevent anyone else from having.

Authors often find themselves addressing a void. They have readers but no feedback, so they are left to wonder if their book buyers actually read the book and apply its contents to their lives or just scan it briefly before putting it aside. So please gather with one or more others to read this short book. Then send me your reactions and actions. This is not just for my own gratification. I'm seeking to apply this foundational principle: nobody alone is as smart as are all of us together.

As you will see, what follows is not a detailed how-to guide or road map. However, if you wish to delve deeper into the topics in this book when you are done reading, you'll find a list of books, articles, and civic groups in the Resources for Action appendix so you can take it to the next level. My goal here is a more modest one: to spark your curiosity and desire enough to alter your routines so that you become one of that tiny percentage of people who, one way or another, make the world go 'round. In the lives of our communities, it is easier than we think to make improvements. Climbing little hills leads to bigger hills and on to little mountains—that's how this book makes more difficult accomplishments easier to contemplate. Just getting started may be your most formidable hurdle, but one that no one can stop you from overcoming.

One additional encouragement: We live in an age of "experts" and "specialists." They said have credentials and credibility. The rest of us are expected to defer to them or be ridiculed. A benefit of seeing yourself through the various roles discussed in this volume is to enhance your own sense of credibility. Identifying as a citizen, consumer, worker, taxpayer, and voter, who has experience as such and is informed, gives you more credibility than just calling yourself a person or individual. It is dismaying when at a public gathering someone says to me, "I'm a nobody, but can you tell me why this is and must be so? Why can't I get some fair treatment or some answers at least?" I usually respond with the words, "Please, nobody is a nobody!" If any readers think of themselves this way, please abandon such self-typecasting and open yourself to the different roles you play in your life. You're a worker, a consumer, a taxpayer, a voter, a parent, a veteran—a citizen. This book seeks to strengthen your own sense of these different roles, and being aware of them will increase your self-confidence, improve your quality of life and that of those around you, and contribute to us all creating a better society.

I, the Citizen

Historians say 495 to 529 BCE, the time of the statesman Pericles, was the golden age of ancient Athenian democracy. The men (women were not allowed to vote, though they found ways to be influential) made an important distinction between Athenians who behaved as "public citizens," caring for and engaging in the city-state of some forty-five thousand voters, and those who cared only for themselves. The latter were called "idiots," or ignorant people, because they didn't improve society. Today, the word "idiot" has taken on a different meaning, so we do not have a popular contemporary noun to describe the great majority of Americans who stay within their private lives and barely venture into the civic square except maybe to cast a vote.

Go down any familiar residential street and count the homes and apartments whose inhabitants show up at town meetings and neighborhood-action gatherings or circulate petitions, not to mention participate in rallies and marches or attend legislative, agency, or courtroom hearings. If you count one in thirty, that would be unusual. The rest will say they are just minding their own business or want to be left alone. They may add that they are not into politics and believe politicians are corrupt or crooks. The problem is that politicians and the giant corporate interests they protect, subsidize, or immunize are always "into" politics and impact our lives. Politics and business lobbyists won't let you alone for a minute. You are breathing their polluted air; drinking and cooking with their contaminated water; being denied services you've paid for, such as health care; being exposed to unsafe drugs and other products; experiencing overbilling; paying for unlawful wars of aggression; being thwarted by crumbling infrastructure, including schools, public transit, bridges, highways, and inadequate clinics; and not being prepared for pandemics and other health crises. You can extend the list, for sure. So if politicians and their corporate paymasters never leave you alone, why do you leave them alone, especially when they're using your sovereign power and consumer dollars against you?

Ever wonder why corporations are always involved in *politics*? Or why single-issue groups are always *into politics* and often get their way, even when their issue is supported by a minority of voters? Ever wonder why 625 drug lobbyists swarmed Congress to keep their taxpayer subsidies and your drug prices sky-high in 2001? Ever wonder why there are thousands of lobbyists and campaign funders wrapping themselves around members of Congress to keep bloating the military budget and the boomerang wars? Weapons companies support military conflicts because war means more profits for them. Ever wonder why banks, finance companies, and credit card giants know the profiles, vulnerabilities, and needs of members of Congress? Take a look at the interest rates you're paying on consumer loans, payday loans, mortgage loans, and unpaid credit card balances.

I call people who wonder, grumble, and still do nothing to confront these wrongdoings and injustices the Apathetics.

In 1948, President Harry S. Truman was expected to lose the election to New York governor Thomas E. Dewey. The polls predicted Dewey would win by 5 to 15 percent. Truman hit the campaign trail by train and traveled thousands of miles—crisscrossing the country from coast to coast, north to south.

Addressing over ninety thousand farmers and their families in a huge field in Dexter, Iowa, he didn't mince words. Here is what "Give 'em hell, Harry" told the farmers that day:

I wonder how many times you have to be hit on the head before you find out who's hitting you? . . . These Republican gluttons of privilege are cold men. They are cunning men. . . . They want a return of the Wall Street economic dictatorship. . . . I'm not asking you just to vote for me. Vote for yourselves!"

Truman won the election by more than three million popular votes and garnered 303 electoral votes compared to Dewey's 189.

Other candidates for public office have had to grapple with the vast number of people, voters and nonvoters alike, who are so disconnected from the impact of concentrated power dynamics that they either stay home or vote against their own interests. They do so little homework to inform their vote that they become bedazzled by the manipulative rhetoric of the candidates they identify with—before these bloviators go back to Congress or their state capitals and betray them.

I had to confront this challenge as a third-party or independent candidate for president in 1996, 2000, 2004, and 2008. Finally, after getting nowhere with my evidence and pleas, I took to satire in 2008 and created the new American Society of Apathetics. In campaign addresses, I declared:

Membership is free and simple, appropriately enough, with no rights because of society's dedication to no exertions whatsoever, except to recite the solemn oath of the Apathetic to yourself, to wit:

"As a member of the American Society of Apathetics, I solemnly swear and declare that I will endure any injustice, accept any abuse, absorb any disrespect, suffer any deprivation, concede any exclusion, inhale any toxics, and avoid any public responsibilities to defend my inalienable right to apathy, so help me, my descendants, and my country."

I added this suggestion:

> If you wish to bond with any other potential Apathetics in your community and not have to exert yourself, please slide to us the relevant web address. The message is therefore communicated automatically without the necessity of lifting your voice to say anything.

In audience after audience, there was a ripple of chuckles and then nothing thereafter. They were not about to self-describe, whether they were there in person or listening or viewing my invitation on radio or TV.

It is very hard, no matter who tries, to break through to the Apathetics, regardless of pleas, exhortations, satire, or aspirational benefits that one would accrue from becoming Active. As my father questioned his children once: "What is the most powerful force in the world?" His answer: the force of apathy. Or, as a quote often misattributed to Edmund Burke, the eighteenth-century Anglo-Irish statesman, reads, "All that is required for evil to prevail is for good men to do nothing."

So, where do those recollections lead us? Back to ancient Athenians' shunning the indifferent among them. Civic indifference starts with a person's lack of self-respect and disregard for the power of civic action. The antidote, the source of real self-regard, is to stand up, stand tall, and call out the rapacious and ravaging forces coming down on communities.

Civic self-respect is another way of describing civic self-motivation: how to achieve that crucial state of mind that propelled Benjamin Franklin to build community institutions that still stand today, drove Frederick Douglass to be a leader against the scourge of human slavery, and motivated Helen Keller to demonstrate the triumph of the human spirit as she advocated for socioeconomic justice and peace. All three engaged in remarkable self-improvement, pursued an expanded purpose in life, and were driven by the prospect of social betterment of their friends, neighbors, and eventually larger communities numbering in the millions.

It starts with individuals saying to themselves: "I want to count. I am a human being wanting to help other human beings in whatever capacity I can—small, medium, or large." Too often people inclined in this direction stop short by saying, "But I'm just one person up against concentrated power or opposition. I can't make a difference."

Here is a nature metaphor I have found to be clarifying. The Mississippi River begins with tiny flows of water in northern Minnesota and Montana. It starts with rivulets that turn into brooks, which in turn become streams, then small rivers, then tributaries, such as the great Missouri River—all of which aggregate into the mighty Mississippi River. Arguably the single greatest natural resource to make America's giant economy, this river started modestly, but with momentum in a singular direction unstoppable by contrary natural forces.

This metaphor has its limitations, of course. But it does suggest how dictators arrive at their domination—authoritarian or totalitarian—over millions of people, century after century. It doesn't matter the state of communications technology, the speed of transportation, or the level of formal education of the people; nor does the presence of a democratic constitution affect events. They become dictators top-down in a stunning sequence of hierarchies of obedience, active or silent, repeated all the way to where people are raising their families and burying their dead. There were, long before, very few "rivulets," and resisters were either jailed, executed, or placed under close surveillance. The soil was in many ways fertile for a strongman takeover, whether through a junta or an election in a country where there is one ruling party. In many countries, few guardrails exist: no independent prosecutors, judicial review, free press, or democratic procedures with deep roots, such as our Bill of Rights and due processes of law.

Let's start with our country: millions of people want to see solutions to what they view as problems but don't know what to do or how to go about righting a wrong. The first crucial step is to develop a public spirit. As the famous judge Learned Hand said in a speech in New York's Central Park about eighty years ago: "Liberty lies in the hearts of men and women; when it dies there, no constitution, no law, no court can ever do much to help it." He included justice and peace in his definition of liberty.

Consider your civic assets. You start out with a big constitutional advantage over giant corporations and their elected politicians. The preamble to the US Constitution reads "We the People," not "We the Elected Officials" nor "We the Corporations." There is no mention in the Constitution of the word *corporation* nor the word *company*. It only refers to "persons." They are given the sovereign power in our republic. Elected officials receive much of your sovereign power to run the government at both the federal and state levels. Therefore every elected politician representing your district, city, town, or village has a piece of the sovereign power that the majority of voters delegated on behalf of all the people. That is one reason you should take politics personally. When millions of Americans protested George W. Bush's and Dick Cheney's criminal devastation of Iraq, there were signs by the marchers saying "Bush/Cheney do not speak for us." They wanted to say out loud that their piece of sovereign power was not part of this criminal invasion, this sociocide of the innocent people of Iraq.

These marchers were entering the first stage of civic engagement—open to all. Our Constitution guarantees this right of free speech, assembly, and petition of one's government in the very first amendment. This first-stage activity has changed the course of American history. Showing up is half of democracy. When our founders showed up in that hot summer of 1776 in Philadelphia, they proclaimed the Declaration of Independence from the tyranny of King George III. Throughout our history, showing up for marches, rallies, demonstrations, picketing, legislative and agency hearings, and court houses has led to the creation of new political parties, unions, farmers' organizations, consumer protections, healthier environments, constitutional amendments abolishing slavery, women's suffrage, the end of the Vietnam War, veteran protests, nuclear arms agreements, and on and on.

The more you read and reflect, the more you start distinguishing between charity and justice. Both are necessary. Charity relieves immediate needs, such as through food kitchens or pantries. Justice is more about prevention, such as an economy that pays workers a living wage or establishes a basic income system so that people do not need to go to food kitchens. A short phrase captures this: "A society that has more justice is a society that needs less charity."

I often say, "Our country has more problems than we should tolerate and more solutions than it uses." Think about this for a moment. Think about structural deprivations or injustices and the ready solutions, some already adopted in one place or another.

Imagine replacing energy from fossil fuels with renewable energy, implementing fairer taxes to address the inequality that favors the big corporations and the superrich, increasing the federal minimum wage so that CEOs are not making more than three hundred to four hundred times what the average worker makes. Making workplaces, schools, hospitals, factories, and mines safer should have broad support.

Practical ideas about expanding community policing, improving public transit, and creating more affordable housing are ready to deploy. The benefits of better consumer protection, drinking water, and clean air are well known but inadequately championed. It is time to upgrade children's nutritional intake and enact Medicare for all.

Enforcing the law against corporate crimes should be a given. Our health and safety laws should be a given. Better safeguards to achieve a more efficient government—one that also controls outsourcing to companies—will benefit taxpayers and free up tax dollars for community necessities. Waging peace instead of war has indisputable benefits.

Best practices can set a floor for improvements in these and in countless other areas.

Place yourself in the civic roles described in this volume and you will realize the potential of greater being and doing, replacing tired routines and tedium with the basic principle of living an active life in a democracy. The whole is greater than the sum of its parts. This is another way of defining healthy, happy, productive communities that allow future generations to prosper and build upon them.

In 1964, together with half a dozen friends and relatives, I picketed the New York Coliseum, which was then hosting the annual automobile show. Our signs, handouts, and interviews made the local television news that evening and launched wider protests against unsafely designed cars, which in turn led to the enactment of lifesaving federal auto and highway safety laws in 1966.

It didn't matter that no one else was picketing elsewhere in the country at the same time. It mattered that we felt a duty to do this for the many friends who were killed or injured because their vehicles had no seat belts, airbags, padded dashboards, nor several other long-available crash protections whose implementation was being ignored by the style- and horsepower-obsessed auto company bosses. And we knew that just about every social-justice movement had started with a conversation between two people.

Political scholars have rarely written about a civic philosophy embraced by those who avoid small talk with people they meet and discuss issues of importance instead. My father was one of them, making the most of visits from all kinds of patrons at his spacious restaurant on Main Street. As the owner of a nearby shoe store once said: "At Nader's a nickel bought you a cup of coffee and ten minutes of political talk." Many social issues were tossed around, catching the attention of the customers and helping area residents get informed and, sometimes, stirred up. In the nearly fifty years he ran the restaurant, as travelers came through town on Route 44, my father educated, motivated, and inspired tens of thousands to think a little more deeply about conditions that affected them locally and around the country and the world. To friends who cautioned him that speaking about controversial issues might cost him business, he replied: "When I sailed past the Statue of Liberty, I took it seriously. Don't you?"

By the time I became a teenager, I noticed there were a few other citizen activists in town. One regular was Mr. Franz, an elderly, white-haired gentleman who was well prepared at town meetings to question or make recommendations to the mayor and selectmen, as they were called. We could always count on him to stand up, holding stacks of paper, and challenge budget items, pending projects, or policies he thought unwise. People treated him as a maverick or oddball, pointing him out when he walked down Main Street, as if to say, "There is the town drunk, the town fool, and the town citizen." Most townspeople habitually abstained from town affairs, leaving their interests to be decided by others, including the owners of the town's big textile factory, among others, and I found it strange that they were the ones considered normal. My parents were delighted and invigorated by these civic and political exchanges. They were so pleased that this little town had a six-day-a-week newspaper—the *Winsted Evening Citizen*. My father left his native Lebanon for America because of the stifling climate under the Ottoman Empire. Their new freedoms were not to be taken for granted but to be exercised. Life in America, they believed, was more than just work, raising children, and enjoying some recreation. Each day was an opportunity to devote some time to civic life.

First-stage civic activity is not necessarily random and reactive. It can become an organized hobby. An especially spectacular example was the career of Russ Kick. Early in life, he discovered Freedom of Information laws—federal and state—and started filing creative requests for government files on many topics. The *New York Times* wrote in his obituary: "Mr. Kick . . . was renowned for using the Freedom of Information Act. He spent two decades publishing tens of thousands of pages of government files, court documents, corporate memos, scientific studies, and covert action reports, all part of a lifelong mission to hold authorities and institutions accountable." David Cuillier, a University of Arizona professor who studies government transparency, said of Kick: "The work he was doing was phenomenal. He showed that anybody in this country could get public records out of the government, even when the government didn't want to give them out."

In the early months of Bush's attack on Iraq, Kick pried from the government's censorious hands hundreds of photographs depicting flag-draped coffins of US soldiers killed there. He broke Washington's self-serving ban on visual records of this war for oil. Coming from a family of voracious readers, Kick taught himself methods of obtaining and anthologizing information. He was a star public citizen and a one-man media generator, the type we'd hoped for when we were lobbying Congress to pass the Freedom of Information Act, in 1974. He passed away at the early age of fifty-two in 2021.

Another example is Dr. John Geyman. He could have retired to much-deserved leisure. He had done it all: family physician, professor of medicine at the University of Washington, editor of journals on family medicine, and head of the activist organization

Physicians for a National Health Program. He chose instead to become a leading civic educator on the horrors of the dangerously commercialized, price-gouging, benefit-denying, billing-fraud-ridden, so-called health care system in the US. Working out of his home, he has authored some twenty books with graphics on just about every profiteering health care sector. He has documented the domination of health care by powerful corporations, which use corrupt political connections in Washington to immunize themselves from law enforcement and reap trillions of dollars in subsidies and inflated billings.

He sends copies of his books to every member of Congress and reporter who cover medicine, patients, hospitals, clinics, and so-called regulatory agencies. Because he speaks truth to greedy power using the clearest narratives, he has received far less media attention than he warrants given his singular role among physicians in America. Dr. Geyman's books gain attention thanks to his evidence-based research and provocative titles: *Profiteering, Corruption and Fraud in US Health Care* (2020), *America's Mighty Medical-Industrial Complex: Negative Impacts and Positive Solutions* (2022), *Crisis in US Health Care: Corporate Power vs. The Common Good* (2017), *Health Care Wars: How Market Ideology and Corporate Power Are Killing Americans* (2012), and *Common Sense: Medicare for All: What Will It Mean for Me?* (2021).

As a Princeton University graduate and a member of the National Academy of Medicine, Geyman could have relaxed around the age of seventy. Now, at ninety-two, he is still putting out material that medical and nursing schools should make required reading. He has written for the general public, whose stake in getting more efficient universal health care—as other Western countries have had for many years—is literally a matter of life and death, especially during epidemics and pandemics. Until his late eighties, he would volunteer to fly cancer patients from Bainbridge Island to Seattle for treatment.

It is because we have a weak democracy dominated by corporate media that Dr. Geyman is not appreciated as a national hero nor featured regularly on the news. This is what happens when there are nowhere near as many rivulets as demanded by the crucial necessities of our times. Nonetheless, Dr. Geyman is not fazed; he continues to perform his duties with civic stamina and knowledge as a volunteer citizen par excellence.

Ed and Joyce Koupal went from stage one to stage two and then to stage three, without stopping, in their drive to deepen the democracy of their home state, California. A used-car salesman with strong opinions about a just society, Ed, along with his wife, got tired of complaining during the governorship of former actor Ronald Reagan. They viewed Reagan as a cruel man with a deceptive smile. A corporate stooge in public office. They discovered a powerful though little-used tool. Voters in California could recall elected officials if they got enough signatures to put this recall power on the ballot and then win the subsequent election. In this case, the recall or dismissal would be directed at Governor Reagan.

They went to work gathering the hundreds of thousands of signatures needed to put the recall on the ballot. They perfected ways to collect signatures efficiently at shopping malls, enlisting hundreds of volunteers in this endeavor. They were getting close enough to qualifying by the due date to warrant a front-page article in the *Wall Street Journal*. But even their Herculean efforts weren't enough due to the short time allowed under the law for gathering the huge number of necessary signatures. Undiscouraged, they looked to enact reforms through the other tool of direct democracy: the initiative. They won one statewide initiative protecting California's coastal ocean and another to establish a state ethics commission to hold politicians accountable. Their movement—called the People's Lobby—was taking on ever more important reforms and attracting attention from citizen groups in other states. Ed worked long days. He was diagnosed with cancer and died in 1976, which took the heart out of the lobby. It tried to continue, but shortly thereafter, Joyce took ill and passed away. Regardless, they had shown what could be done by using the levers of direct democracy that industries such as Big Tobacco had misused for years to weaken or block laws for the people.

Lois Gibbs was minding her own business as a wife and mother of three children in Love Canal, a neighborhood in the city of Niagara Falls. Unbeknownst to the hundreds of working-class homeowners, beneath their houses were the remains of a chemical-waste dump abandoned by the Hooker Chemical Company before developers covered it with soil and built housing. Lois and other mothers noticed their kids developing strange ailments. Ultimately, the whole dangerous scene was exposed in the media. Lois became the spokesperson for her neighborhood, speaking to the rush of reporters and working with her neighbors to demand action from the New York Department of Health and the Environmental Protection Agency. She became a leader out of the necessity to protect her own and other exposed children in the community. After the authorities evacuated the area and paid some compensation, Lois moved to a Virginia suburb near Washington, D.C., and started a group now called the Center for Health, Environment & Justice. She was soon drawing crowds of worried parents all over the country, and the number of citizen chapters of the center grew into the hundreds. Her biennial conventions hosted energetic exchanges of information and stories of local victories over the polluters and their formerly silent violence against innocents. It became the leading grassroots movement against toxics in America's neighborhoods. Lois Gibbs took "I, the Citizen" through all three stages: pressing lawmakers to enact laws, engaging lawyers to bring and win lawsuits, and starting a new group to expose corporate toxics and cover-ups as well as coordinate cleanups of toxic-waste sites.

A similar experience—this time the loss of a daughter to a drunk driver—enraged Candace Lightner, who launched

Mothers Against Drunk Driving and built it into a widely covered national organization pushing for stronger laws and penalties against drunk drivers. Lightner said to the *Washington Post* that she started the organization because she was "very mad, . . . very bitter, there were elements of revenge." She moved quickly from the first to the second to the third stage of citizen action.

At the local level, there are thousands of these active citizen volunteers holding their communities' sinews of justice together. Often they work without fanfare or media recognition. They stem the tides of political and governmental decay, of corporate greed and recklessness, in quiet pursuit of what the majority of the passive citizenry wants and deserves. Sometimes they support candidates running in school- or planning-board elections who support the local Industrial Areas Foundation agenda or pursue their causes through local referenda. Ernesto Cortés Jr. is a senior adviser with the Industrial Areas Foundation. Like many protégés of the venerable community organizer Saul Alinsky, who started the foundation, Cortés believes the key to building civic power is to teach the powerless to effectively participate in public life.

Often people in urban communities read about these valiant citizens in obituaries and, in effect, say to themselves, "I didn't know about this person doing all these courageous things." That is because we do not have a democratic media owned and controlled by the people. We will never have a thriving democracy so long as we have a corporate media, increasingly driven by the hedge funds that buy up chains of newspapers and strip-mine them of reporters and resources needed to provide the stories and alerts readers need. There needs to be more "I, the Citizens" in communities who make sure that there is at least a weekly paper in smaller towns and villages and who rally larger urban communities to support a thriving press. Newspapers produce most of the content that is taken by radio and television or finds its way onto social media. Almost everyone likes a community newspaper, so you will find a broad coalition of support for such an institution, including people in the business, education, labor, recreation, and health care sectors.

The more you converse with people around you, the more you begin to realize that there is a deep mismatch between the people and the government institutions and lobbyists around them. People connect once in a while—by voting, asking for specific services, complaining, and petitioning—while the governmental agencies and the highly paid lobbyists are at it full time. It is no contest. That's the asymmetry that plagues the practice of democracy. That's why in the 1960s we started full-time citizen action groups to countervail the axis of government and business lobbying. It's also why, right after World War I, like-minded citizens started the permanent institutions known as the National Association for the Advancement of Colored People and the American Civil Liberties Union, to champion civil rights for all. These two groups' roles in combating the practices of bigotry and defending free speech have been historic. Their work locally and nationally supports my belief that there can be no daily democracy without daily citizenship. There are presently huge vacuums where the axis of government and business does what it wants because no civic institutions are taking them on day in and day out. Very few citizen watchdogs allow major abuses to continue unchallenged. The bloated, wasteful military budget; the hundreds of billions looted through computerized billing fraud of consumers; the thousands of Americans who die every week in hospitals from preventable problems; the spoiling of public lands; the domination of the public airwaves by radio and TV companies; the absence of scrutiny regarding trillions of dollars in government contracts and grants to commercial companies—these are just a few examples of how these vested interests are commandeering what belongs to the people.

Your curiosity continues its journey, leading you to sit in on some political campaign events that allow questions from the audience. Listening to the candidates, you note how few issues they speak about and how they tend toward temporary relief of people's distress without going to the roots. A candidate may espouse the need for more robust and nutritious food programs for kids and adults without addressing the frozen minimum wage and the need to raise it to levels at which people can afford to buy their food.

When question time comes, you see how low voters' expectations are. They largely respond to the narrow issue framework and palliatives emerging from the candidates' remarks. There are no questions, for example, about why Western European countries have all these social safety nets and family facilities while we, the wealthiest country in the world, don't. Nor are there answers to some of the most fundamental questions relating to universal health insurance, reining in giant corporations, establishing a Department of Peace, or public funding of public campaigns. These are just some of the questions that came to you from your reading and pondering after you decided to incorporate civic activity into your routine. You now understand that keeping voter expectations narrow and low is a controlling tactic by many candidates. They speak generally about the American dream, but you must live in a nightmare to believe them.

One customary way to keep expectation levels low for presidential, congressional, and gubernatorial candidates is to have a distraction agenda of intense emotional content. At a campaign event you say, under your breath, "Get back to the basics, politician." Then you find yourself standing up and saying this in public to the candidate on the stage. Many eyes look at you favorably as you give examples. You are changing the dynamics of the gathering, shifting it more to the audience, which starts moving from passivity to activity. At the conclusion, more people may come up to you than to the candidate, who is whisked off by his nervous handlers to the next meet-and-greet event of empty promises and gestures.

What starts to dawn on you is that being a citizen is not just an impulse; you become more skilled and effective the more you do it. People learn how to be a skilled electrician, carpenter, lawyer, doctor, social worker, nurse, physician, bridge player, or swimmer by reading, thinking, and practicing. Becoming a skilled citizen is no different except for two aspects—*one*, anybody can be a skilled citizen, and *two*, nobody can fire a skilled citizen under our Constitution.

This realization prompts a thunderous question: how can 535 lawmakers in Congress, using the people's power, control hundreds of millions of citizens on behalf of a few hundred corporations? Answer: not enough daily citizenship. The next question pops into your head quite naturally: how much daily citizenship is needed for major victories? You dig into history books old and new and see it is hard to find any answers.

Here is my experience: When 1 percent, or sometimes less, of the citizenry becomes active on an important reform, they can change the national direction by meeting three criteria: One, they know what they're talking about and are accurate and detailed when they communicate. Two, their proposed reform is or can be supported by most of the American people. Three, they focus their popular demands directly on the forum that is authorized to enact the legislation. Less than 1 percent can mean as little as a thousand people from all 435 congressional districts combined, which is what it took to enact legislation on consumer protection bills in the 1960s regarding auto safety and meat and poultry inspection laws.

If the composition of Congress becomes less responsive, it will take more citizen power. These activists would agree to put in volunteer time and raise the modest funds to retain one full-time lobbyist/organizer, who would build support within the congressional district among the local and state-level representatives, social and religious groups, and others, to put pressure on the congressperson and senators. The more significant the demonstrated and determined support for a popular citizen agenda, the more likely the mass media will cover citizen demands, especially if the number of declared supportive senators and representatives keeps increasing. One percent of the citizenry is about 2.5 million adults. Two of the most powerful lobbies in the US—the National Rifle Association and the American Israel Public Affairs Committee—have the backing of enough members of Congress to get their positions easily accepted. Neither of these groups has more than 250,000 activists putting in the time back in their congressional districts.

When young students in schools grow up learning how to be powerless, there is a likely tendency as they grow older to exaggerate what it takes to turn Congress around. Remember, there are just 535 lawmakers, and if you make them choose, they'll want your votes—and no primary challenges—far more than they'll want campaign dollars from vested interests.

If this all sounds too rosy, you can find out for yourself by going to the historical record. I stressed this point in my small paperback *Breaking Through Power: It's Easier Than We Think*. One of my major suggestions was a formal summons—to be sent by organized citizens to their senators or representatives—to show up in person to town meetings run by the citizens who are presenting their proposed legislation, backed by evidence and lively rhetoric. Lawmakers could be told in advance of the issues, so they can prepare their responses before sharing with the public and the media in attendance. The formal summons is printed in Appendix I at the end of this book. You can see how it turns the dynamic of initiation from the legislator over to the people, whose sovereign power befits such a status.

Because so few people typically turn out for public meetings with members of Congress or state legislators, my guess is that five hundred clear petition signatures with the signers' occupations and emails will get a US representative to your town meeting. Probably anywhere from a thousand to two thousand signatures, depending on the size of the state, will draw a US senator in person to your meeting. The effort must be done with some formality, dignity, and comprehensiveness. Note the unused talent in each congressional district that has colleges, universities, or community colleges, as well as more than a few retired people with time and experience and all kinds of other talents.

One reason people all over the world like democracy is that it brings the best out of the people. However, democracy provides more legal rights and remedies for the people than the citizens use. This is an important point because people acting for change often stress accurately the need for new or upgraded rights and remedies without also striving to get people to use the rights they already have—such as voting, running for elected office, organizing marches, qualifying popular referendums, filing lawsuits, and many others. Furthermore, there is the frequent situation of obstructive lawmakers erecting costly discriminatory hurdles to overcome before the people can exercise the rights they do have.

A case in point is the right of third parties and independent candidates to appear on the local, state, and national ballot lines alongside those of the Republican and Democratic Parties. Apart from some recent spurts enabled by court decisions, we have been going backward—from the easy days of the first half of the nineteenth century, when candidates merely had to print their ballots, to the present day, when a jungle of obstacles has been put into place by the two-party duopoly to create a noncompetitive electoral system that deprives voters of more choices and voices.

Back in 1985, Richard Winger took a citizen's interest in the exclusion of minor party candidates. He started by reading the history: many states had made ballot access unattainable by reducing the short window of time to gather verifiable petition signatures, which effectively imposed a prohibitive cost on supporters. He also learned that it was far more difficult to get onto the ballot here than in Canada or any other Western country. More signatures by far were required in states such as Texas, North Carolina, and California than were required in entire nations abroad. He became incensed and started the newsletter *Ballot Access News* from his kitchen table in San Francisco. Now, thirty-eight years later, he has become a legend and a field-leading expert, learning and writing more than any university professor about the intricate laws, regulations, and lawsuits in all the states. He knows all about the state ballot access laws and the ways they restrict voters' choices by blocking third-party or independent candidates. Over and over again, he shows that when we lower barriers for third-party candidates, voters increase their bargaining power vis-à-vis the two-party duopoly. *Ballot Access News* is now the gold standard for providing regular, up-to-date information month after month on the topic (see ballot-access.org). Richard is not getting rich from his subscription income but he has made a modest living serving hundreds of citizen groups, public-election officials, election-reform lawyers, the media, and curious citizens. Always willing to answer written or phone inquiries for free, Richard can be considered a supercitizen in this important field of expanding our choices to create a more competitive democracy. Instead of being cowed by the impediments and the great odds against reform, Winger took advantage of doing what nobody could stop him from doing. "I, the Citizen" should always keep this point in mind: start with the things that nobody can stop you from doing.

For example, suppose during your conversations about presidential, congressional, and statewide elections, you get from many people you speak to a common, concrete sense of what they think they deserve from the candidates. Start with what they should expect from the president of the United States. Together, you agree to make a list of what that vastly powerful position and the departments and agencies of the executive branch should be delivering and striving to deliver. This gets to the point of higher expectations, which liberates voters from the customary manipulations by politicians using rhetoric and euphemisms such as "peace through strength" or "Make America Great Again." The more informed our expectations are, the more power shifts to the citizenry for shaping the electoral agenda. One likely place to start is with election reform and public funding. Another is moving to give the people *control* of what the people *own*, i.e., the commons currently under corporate control, as I will explain later. You can put these discussions and lists of more immediate livelihood demands on the internet for further diffusion around the country. Nobody can stop you from doing these things. Not yet anyway!

Having read this far, you may be seeking advice on how to keep up your morale and optimism and ward off feelings of despair or discouragement. Let's start with a baseball metaphor. Suppose someone told you that the Yankees just defeated their opponent by a score of 138 to 0. You would think the Bronx Bombers were the superstars of baseball history—until you learn that there were only two ballplayers on the other team who had to do the pitching, catching, fielding, and hitting. Always ask yourself, when figuring the odds of getting change started and noticed by the public, how many "good guys" are on the playing field. For example, how many full-time citizens are now starting to push members of Congress to require the Pentagon to obey an existing federal law mandating that all federal departments and agencies submit an auditable budget to Congress every year? Answer: zero. Not one person. The Pentagon has violated this law since 1992. An audit is the first step toward saving huge amounts of taxpayer dollars. So doesn't that change your sense of feasibility for getting this issue—stuck on Capitol Hill—moving? Every secretary of defense has promised to provide auditable budgets, usually with a four-year lead time. Yet it doesn't get done.

Whether the subject for change is federal, state, or local, always ask how many full-time citizen advocates are working on these changes. You would be surprised how few are needed to get some movement and media underway on clear-cut abuses, corruption, or delays. So the first task is getting just a few more people working on it, and that awareness keeps the "it ain't gonna happen" attitude, along with the corresponding pessimism, at bay.

By now you may be receptive to a more formidable power to keep you going; to keep you determined and resilient and make you stronger as you experience hurdles or bumps along the way. That power is what I call an ever-maturing "civic personality." Just as an "athletic personality" and a relentless will to win marks the difference between athletes of comparable physical skills, so too is the case in the civic arena.

A good way to learn about what makes up a civic personality is by reading biographies of civic leaders throughout history or articles about how civic advocates achieved their victories. Benjamin Franklin had one of the greatest, most creative civic personalities in American history. Reading biographies of Franklin and his many institutional creations—lending libraries, volunteer fire departments, post offices, colleges, and much more—can be motivational, especially given how he started as a penniless youth, sailing from his native Boston to Philadelphia. His unfinished autobiography, in the form of a letter to his son, is a must-read for all schoolchildren who want to learn good habits and self-improvement.

Reading is one thing, but muscling up your own civic personality is another, and it has to come from your own willingness to absorb relevant information, learn from your past mistakes, keep in mind the big picture but also tend to daily details without delay, and sharpen your stamina and resiliency without diverting from healthy living habits. I knew some terrific civic leaders— good character and personality—who neglected their need for sleep and good nutrition and who smoked cigarettes hour after hour, shortening their life span. There are other facets of strong civic personalities. You share or give credit generously, admit your mistakes, have an open mind for revisions, avoid losing your temper no matter the provocation, respect the learning curve of newcomers, understand what is required to lead by example, keep thinking in new ways, and believe that a strategy, tactic, rebuttal, or slogan is always somewhere out there in the ether to be grasped at a moment of illumination or serendipity.

Speaking of serendipity, let's envision you're reading Walter Isaacson's biography of Benjamin Franklin and come upon these words by Franklin on page 474:

> I wish to be useful even after my death, if possible, in forming and advancing other young men that may be serviceable to their country.

Doesn't that remarkable sense of legacy, of the future, stimulate some thoughts about how you could project your own legacy far ahead and become an ever better ancestor, bringing the best out of people long after you're gone?

Franklin was an unparalleled master of motivation, self-taught skills, and self-improvement. His personal traits complimented his efforts to improve the civic community. Sensing a public need, he immediately read, convened, and put solutions into practice. He was amazingly prolific. Isaacson jammed some of the solutions he came up with into one paragraph:

> He was, during his eighty-four-year-long life, America's best scientist, inventor, diplomat, writer, and business strategist, and he was also one of its most practical, though not most profound, political thinkers. He proved by flying a kite that lightning was electricity, and he

invented a rod to tame it. He devised bifocal glasses and clean-burning stoves, charts of the Gulf Stream and theories about the contagious nature of the common cold. He launched various civic improvement schemes, such as a lending library, college, volunteer fire corps, insurance association, and matching grant fund-raiser. He helped invent America's unique style of homespun humor and philosophical pragmatism. In foreign policy, he created an approach that wove together idealism with balance-of-power realism. And in politics, he proposed seminal plans for uniting the colonies and creating a federal model for a national government. . . .

He had faith in the wisdom of the common man and felt that a new nation would draw its strength from what he called "the middling people." Through his self-improvement tips for cultivating personal virtues [his *Poor Richards Almanac* was a global bestseller in some one hundred languages] and his civic-improvement schemes for furthering the common good, he helped to create, and to celebrate, a new ruling class of ordinary citizens.

Yet Franklin was also a human being. For all his achievements, he was a real person, someone afflicted with bouts of depression, who started out as a poor apprentice printer with only two years of formal education and had trouble with arithmetic. Franklin enjoyed life—social gatherings, good food, wry humor, arguments and differences of opinion, poking fun at pomp and ceremony, and constantly wrestling with the all-encompassing goal of producing the good life for all.

For Franklin, participation in society was shaped by his character and personality, which he challenged himself to improve and measured via his famous daily accounting of his accomplishments and adherence to various virtues. His schedule ran from the time he woke up to the time he went to sleep. He did this without obsession, having taught himself a philosophy of routine zest and absorbing curiosity.

Whether on foreign missions representing his country before the French and English ruling classes or deep in negotiations over the creation of the American republic and its Constitution, he would always describe himself as "B. Franklin, printer."

May the spirit and diverse productivity of Benjamin Franklin stay with the readers of this small volume as a compass, magnet, and anchor whenever consistency of purpose is hindered by hesitancy or loss of self-confidence.

As you develop deeper recognition of and begin asserting yourself in these various roles, you'll become an undeclared "influencer" in your interactions with family, friends, and neighbors—perhaps even in larger circles in the community. Today, *influencer* has a commercial connotation, but I intend it to mean a wiser person to whom others informally reach out for advice and guidance and to open doors. That would include your children, grandchildren, nephews, and nieces who, though clutching their iPhones, still yearn for that comforting, guiding arm around the shoulder.

Place yourself in the expressive roles described in this volume—at your own pace—and you'll generate a sense of greater "being and doing," replacing tired routines and tedium with that basic principle of living an active democratic life: that the whole is greater than the sum of its parts. You'll find you're healthier, happier, and living in more productive communities beside people who live, work, and raise their families to embrace the kind of living democracy that future generations can benefit from and build upon.

As I have repeated often, you cannot have a daily democracy without daily citizenship. Democracy is not a spectator sport. My mother used to convey a sense of our personal and civic responsibility by saying, "I believe it's *you!*" Right on!

CHAPTER TWO

I, the Worker

Workers in a number of large companies are pushing for safer workplace conditions, higher pay, and better benefits. Surprisingly, many workers are not led by existing trade unions seeking to expand their numbers. Various new organizing efforts are more spontaneous and seem to be proceeding to union elections on the energy of the workers themselves. Starbucks, Amazon, and some national fast-food chains are seeing their employees—long passive, resigned, or resigning—staying on in the face of union-busting muscle by giant employers and superrich bosses. Most of these workers are young, under forty years of age. Quite a few are college-educated and were driven to such jobs because of the lack of better opportunities. The new organizing drives are in part bolstered by the labor shortage.

After decades of steadily declining union membership since the early 1970s, this is a welcome development. However, winning a union election and surviving a challenge by the employer in court or before the National Labor Relations Board is still a long way from securing an adequate union contract. The US has the lowest rate of unionized workers in the Western world—about 6 percent of private sector workers and 31 percent of public sector workers. A major reason is that we have the most robust anti-union organizing laws in the Western world, including the 1947 Taft-Hartley Act that, among other restrictions, bans both a "card check" and secondary boycotts. There are other reasons for the decrease in union members: a Democratic Party that takes labor unions for granted and many bureaucratic union leaders who have neither the energy nor the vision to expand. There are exceptions. But one unionist's description of many union presidents as "old, tired, timid, and overpaid" is not far off the mark.

So, what are ordinary workers to do besides continue to perform their jobs and hope for an occasional raise? For most American workers, finding a way to pay an unanticipated $1000 medical bill would be very difficult. That's another way of saying they are living paycheck to paycheck. Many work for bosses of large or midsize companies who make on average three hundred to four hundred times their wages. The multiple was about thirty-five times in 1980. The sky's the limit for overpaid CEOs with rubber-stamp boards of directors. If you're an Apple retail worker making $20 or $22 an hour, how do you feel about your CEO making $833 a minute in 2022, not counting lavish benefits? I've mentioned this disparity before to numerous audiences of various types of workers. Their answer is a shrug of the shoulders. Que será, será.

Compared to workers in France, American laborers are seriously lacking in solidarity. They've passively bought into the discredited capitalist theory of market determinism. Whether it is their economic plight—American labor's frozen wages are about equal to 1978 levels—or the avarice of their bosses, that's what the market decides. Nonsense, says the French working class. When France's truck drivers or members of other labor sectors shut down the highways or an important economic sphere to protest and demand a better livelihood or to not lose some of what they have, public opinion polls show the rest of the laboring class largely supports them. Surprisingly, Reuters reports, "French trade unions are highly influential despite their feeble numbers. At just 8 percent, the number of workers who are union cardholders is one of Europe's lowest." The social safety net in France has, however, historically been much stronger than in the US. France's child protection and other profamily laws, as well as worker protections, are robust.

So, how can a worker go about fighting the odds here, becoming freer to stand up and speak out without jeopardizing employment? Let's start uncontroversially. There is a long history of suggestion boxes, which workers can use to suggest all kinds of ideas to improve efficiency, promote health and safety, decrease turnover, diminish workplace injuries, increase customer satisfaction, reduce spoilage, and advance recycling. Management recognizes that people on the job daily can be an invaluable resource, even for boosting the bottom line. Accepting named or anonymous suggestions in such a box is something all sizable places of work or franchised chain stores can do on their own.

Where would a worker learn about the history of suggestion boxes? Through books. This is a simple way to start building worker power. Reading labor history, not just of labor-management conflicts but also of best practices by other companies in your line of work, opens many windows. It is one thing to urge a boss to do something because it is the right, safe, more profitable, and fairer thing to do. It is quite another to show your boss that another company is doing it better and getting ahead as a result.

There are numerous books, blogs, and biographies about what you can call best practices. They provide more humane policies on restroom breaks, lunchtime, paid sick and family leave, workplace safety, hygiene, air circulation, and more. In the US, astonishingly enough, there is no universal government guarantee for paid maternity leave or paid vacation time. Moreover, many companies have inferior daycare services. Often there's no guaranteed employer-paid health care. Unless you are a union member, you're on your own.

There are various ways to improve the likelihood that the decision-makers at your workplace will listen to you. First, you may be on friendly terms with your manager, who can take your advice up to higher levels in the company. After all, a happy workplace, studies show, leads to either more profits, reduced expenses, or both.

Second, you can make yourself someone who can't be pushed around due to your hard-to-replace work output or your contacts with the local media and citizen groups—or just by your demeanor. You are part of the company team and not just a disposable worker, easy to fire and replace. Finally, conveying that you know what your rights are under local, state, and federal law will give pause to any boss thinking you are easy to ignore or lay off. (The drive to unionize will be treated later.)

Managers look for rank-and-file workers to promote to the next rung, such as supervisor or foreperson. If you demonstrate your value, you will not be viewed as expendable and will be treated as an asset. Good, ambitious workers are not easy to find in any workplace.

By now, you may be asking what relevance this has for a worker's role in strengthening a democratic society. Aren't my examples just ways for a worker to improve their livelihood and that of their fellow workers? You're right, there is a distinction between the personal improvement of working conditions and those of all workers. Putting forces in motion beyond the individual workplace benefits all workers and society at large. Practicing what you preach is an important first step in building a better world.

An interesting recent example of what I mean was published in the January 2023 issue of the *Capitol Hill Citizen*. A reporter met a Starbucks worker who had something significant on her mind. She wasn't pleased, to say the least, with working conditions. But that wasn't what she wanted to talk about. She wished to convey that she hated working there because "every day I'm pumping junk into my fellow Americans' bodies, making them sick. And it makes me sick that I have to do it. . . . Starbucks's products are loaded with caffeine and sugar. It's the perfect combination to create an addiction. It includes drinks that are given to children. . . . There is a reason they don't list the venti calories. And that reason is they don't want people to know. It's more than 500 calories per cup."

Then she proceeds to prove her point: "A venti—or large—peppermint mocha has *ten tablespoons of syrup* in it. Just under half of the cup is filled with syrup. Then there are espresso shots and steamed milk. Then sweetened whipping cream. It's the equivalent of sixteen teaspoons of sugar in each cup. It's more than five hundred calories per cup."

This worker is not finished: "The amount of food that is wasted is shocking. . . . At the end of the day, all the leftover food is thrown out. Expensive sandwiches, nice breads, sandwiches made from quality free-range meats . . . it's thrown out and thrown out and thrown out." This story made its way to consumer groups working for safe, nutritious food. Consumer advocates were further fortified by the disclosures of this courageous worker.

Let's talk about unions. Although the union membership rate of 20 percent in 1983 dropped to 10 percent in 2022, support for unions rose to 71 percent of the general public in 2022, according to Gallup's annual Work and Education survey. This is the highest level of support since 1965.

This surge is a result of the stagnation of inflation-adjusted wages since the seventies and the explosion in executive compensation over the same period. Other trends that have caused increased sympathy for unionization include a rise in surveillance of the white-collar workplace, including remote work; fewer publicized stories of union-leadership corruption; and the exporting of jobs overseas.

All this provides you with a climate in which to better assert your role as a worker inside and outside your place of employment. Labor historians have found that unions' collective bargaining for better contracts favorably influences the wages and working conditions of larger nonunion workplaces. This was especially true after World War II. In 1964, about 34 percent of US workers were in unions.

Even within giant companies and chains, gains in one shop or store can ripple out to the much larger number of nonunion shops or stores. Back in 1997, workers organized just one Starbucks in Canada for a seventy-five-cent wage increase (about a 10 percent raise). Starbucks Canada promptly expanded the increase to all its workers in its ninety-four other nonunion stores, probably to head off any incentive for these laborers to organize their stores.

If you are working to make products or deliver services that have a significant impact on the health, safety, and economic well-being of the public—and if you are bringing your conscience to work—it helps to know where to go for help. For example, Ed Gregory was a veteran assembly line inspector in the late sixties for the General Motors Chevrolet plant in St. Louis. His warnings about a product defect were not heeded by his superiors. Cars were rolling off the assembly lines with a problem that could result in fatal collisions. He saw me on network television testifying before Congress about auto manufacturers producing unsafe vehicles. He called me to describe his detailed warnings, which proved very accurate. We went to the press, causing 6.5 million Chevrolets to be recalled for remediation.

A more formal outlet for workers' consciences opened up in 1986, when amendments were made to the False Claims Act. The amendments allow a person with inside knowledge (individuals, including civil servants, competitors, consultants, or contractors, among others) who discover fraud against the federal government by corporate contractors or other perpetrators of waste, fraud, and corruption to sue the agency or department and request that the Department of Justice take the case. If the DOJ does so and recovers some or all the monies at stake, the person who exposes the misdeed (called the relator) is entitled to a sizable percentage of the recovery (as much as 15 to 30 percent) as a reward for their courage. This money becomes an incentive for others to step forward with their evidence of corporate overcharges or misuse of government funds in a variety of programs.

Being alert to such opportunities and reading, watching, or listening to the news daily can reinforce your value systems and your own sense of self-worth. With the advent of more computerized, impersonal workplaces, workers are extending their job gratification desires beyond pay, benefits, and safety to demand that their managers treat them with dignity and respect.

Scholars have taken note of this shift. It was forecast in a book published in 1999 by two professors, Richard B. Freeman and Joel Rogers, titled *What Workers Want*, based on extensive surveys of workers and their experience in the field of labor-management relations. This book was written before the iPhone/internet revolution, which eased the quick transmission of worker revelations to a wider public for corrective action. Don't think you are being a snitch. Whistleblower rights have advanced tremendously in law and public approval in the last fifty years. There is even a federal Merit Systems Protection Board to deal with retaliation taken by government managers against federal workers. There are also state and federal laws that make it unlawful to punish workers who point out violations of, for instance, environmental pollution control laws.

Our staff and colleagues started the whistleblower revolution with a historic conference in 1972 in Washington, where scores of workers from business, government, and unions shared their experiences about when they courageously went public with their knowledge of corporate and government wrongdoing. We made numerous recommendations in our book about the conference that subsequently found their way into law or public acceptance, including vigorous approval of standout performances that caused risks to careers and reputations. Nowadays, articles on abuses in business, government, and other institutions, such as universities, often come from whistleblowers—just workers with a conscience and empathy who want to protect innocent people from harm. Whistleblowing is an act of a person who, believing that the public interest overrides the interest of the organization they serve, blows the whistle on corrupt, illegal, fraudulent, or harmful activity. It is like applying the golden rule to the people inside and outside an institution who are unknowingly harmed or cheated by a practice, product, or service.

Workers in our country are largely left in the shadows by the mainstream media. When the pandemic-era heroics of, for example, nurses, transport workers, and emergency technicians could not be ignored and were profiled in print and on television and radio, public opinion soared in their favor. But that was an exceptional period of visible crisis. Most of the time, workers are not given their critical due in keeping the country running, while the big bosses claim the limelight and the credit.

What workers know about their craft or skill and how their workplace functions defines much of our country's well-being. They know, for instance, where toxic pollution is being dumped, who is being cheated or lied to, where taxpayers' money is being wasted on corporate contracts, and what sorts of problems have arisen with their company's products. Whether part of a company or self-employed, electricians, plumbers, carpenters, painters, and other craftspeople know what many other Americans need or want to know about products, installations, health and safety, rip-offs, and best performances. They have crucial knowledge to be put to use. Still, the combination of all-too-infrequent whistleblowers, regulatory oversight, and media exposés can't keep up with the devious schemes against workers by companies and trade associations and their opportunistic corporate lawyers.

The history of workers' struggle for justice starts with shared workplace travesties, followed by conversations and meetings outside the workplace. This broadens their frame of reference to include more awareness of class consciousness and solidarity. Additional information about what the corporations and bosses were exploiting and violating stokes productive indignation. Some workers form book clubs; others start union newspapers and distribute pamphlets to spread the word far and wide. They see they are not alone in being mistreated, and that workers in other industries have their own stories to relate. Unfortunately, the plight of workers often goes unreported by the commercial media and is rarely the subject of congressional hearings.

However, after significant gains in workers' pay and benefits, as well as unionization from some heavy industries (auto, steel, and coal mining) between the end of World War II and the seventies, a momentous decrease in worker well-being and security began, unabated to this day. Democratic presidents did not make labor issues a priority; indeed, Bill Clinton opened the door to "pull-down" trade agreements that undermined environmental and labor protections (the North American Free Trade Agreement and the World Trade Organization) and led to the transfer of factories to China and other low-wage autocratic nations. Republican presidents—Nixon, Ford, Reagan, the two Bushes—actively fostered antilabor abuses and policies here in the US under their convenient, cruel market fundamentalism.

When all the parts of this historic slide against labor are aggregated, their collective devastation should provoke a big-time renewal of worker conversations and meetings outside the workplace.

It is hard, even for a close observer of relations between workers and management, to keep in daily memory all the savage and greedy corrosions of worker protections and working-class livelihoods. This loss of power year after year has registered at the level of economic productivity, with data showing that the return on capital is regularly outpacing the return from labor as a percentage of gross domestic product. Thus, the top 1 percent's grab of the nation's wealth has more than doubled since 1980, and the average compensation for CEOs at major corporations has catapulted over the last forty years, from about 35 times the salary of an average worker at their company to 300 to 450 times more—a clear sign of runaway inequality.

Now I'm going to describe briefly the hand that's been dealt to the American worker in the last sixty years, reversing a modest upward trend that occurred in the three postwar decades. See if this rundown gets you steamed before this chamber of horrors is complete.

The federal minimum wage, now at $7.25 an hour, has been essentially frozen. Union membership has declined from about 33 percent of workers in the private sector to a low of 6 percent, while corporate profits have been soaring. Union-busting consulting firms hired by management are getting bored with their success, which is enabled by the weakest labor-protection laws in the Western world. The notorious Taft-Hartley Act of 1947 is still on the books, untouched, as the most anti-union organizing law among Western—and many non-Western—nations. The Occupational Safety and Health Act, enacted by Congress in 1970, has no felony provision for criminal acts that kill workers and is shockingly underfunded and underenforced. State-level workers' compensation laws are similarly shorn of adequate awards, inspectors, and enforcement. Workers going to court for remedies have been obstructed by so-called tort "reform" laws (I call them tort "deform" laws) pushed by the insurance companies, affording the wrongdoing tortfeasors limited liability if not immunity for harmful acts. In a land full of corporate crooks, how many do you see incarcerated and putting on prison stripes?

Corporations and their devious attorneys have tied up workers in contractual knots and stripped them of many freedoms in the so-called "land of the free, home of the brave." To handcuff workers, corporate bosses threaten to or actually do move factories abroad. With all this leverage, they make workers sign contracts so full of inscrutable fine print that many workers do not even know they have agreed to: a noncompete restriction preventing them, for example, from getting a new job at a competing fast-food chain; a nondisparagement clause censoring any criticism of an employer or ex-employer (a gag on free speech that no federal or state government can constitutionally impose onworkers); various kinds of waivers preventing workers from holding wrongdoers accountable for inflicting harm; clauses making it difficult for workers to get back some of the $60 billion in wage theft each year; and clauses subjecting workers to a biased mandatory arbitration for any dispute they may have with an employer without recourse to the courts. One-sided franchise agreements between major national chains and franchisees nationwide are similarly onerous.

Moreover, the traditional defined benefit pension plan, where you get a certain amount per month on retirement, has been mostly replaced with more speculative and uncertain 401(k) plans with trapdoors that have stunned families young and old with loss of anticipated postretirement benefits.

Millions of workers are stripped of minimum wage protection, employer Social Security contributions, unemployment compensation rights, and many other benefits because corporations classify certain employees as independent contractors in the expanding so-called gig economy. On top of all these degradations, surveillance of workers in the workplace or working remotely makes George Orwell's novel *1984* an understatement. Corporate Big Brother is watching and quantifying you all the time. Anxiety, dread, and fear are the common currency of these global corporations astride the planet that control capital, labor, technology, and governments. People know corporations are getting away with more abuses and greed than ever before as they plunder the local, state, and federal treasuries for corporate subsidies, handouts, and bailouts and pay ever fewer taxes, paying off politicians instead and even shaping questions on polls to avoid asking you what you think about their outlawry. They know that fair polls would register high left–right worker support for fundamental changes and basic shifts of power back to workers to redress the huge shift of power away from workers over the decades.

Every day, millions of nurses experience big health care companies making them care for more patients per nurse, under harrowing pressures and paperwork, while the corporate bosses increase their profits. They witness corporate efforts to de-skill their profession with less experienced lower-paid replacements. The giant, profit-glutted railroads are pushing workers to zero— openly predicting autonomous freight trains with more than a hundred cars and no human operators. They are now down to only two workers for trains of that size—a disclosure that more Americans, especially in low-income neighborhoods, alongside the tracks, are discovering, since the Norfolk Southern derailment in eastern Ohio that spilled toxic chemicals, one of a thousand or so of its kind per year. The railroad executives are determined to lobby the feeble federal government to keep even the modest existing regulations from being strengthened as well as bent on disinvesting in repairs and upkeep in favor of stock buybacks, heavier and longer trains, and lavish executive compensation.

By now you may feel overloaded. Don't withdraw from the fight to extend the historical efforts for and by workers to band together for greater workplace rights. It is vital to stop the aggregate mistreatment of millions of workers who keep the country running 24-7. Remember, when it comes to influencing Congress or state legislatures, votes of workers outnumber the votes companies can muster.

Many of the slams against workers may not affect you or other working people immediately—either because you aren't changing jobs or earn much more than the minimum wage, for example. But almost all nonunionized American workers regularly feel deprivations that do not exist in Western European countries and Canada. In these countries, all workers get paid sick and family leave and paid vacation time, for instance. Then there is paid maternity and paternity leave, paid childcare, and, of course, the big one: universal health insurance for everyone.

These are absent from America's social safety net, thanks to the handiwork of corporate lobbyists and their toady politicians. As you focus on the deprivations of the American workplace, you see how these injustices have cost lives, caused poverty, inflicted pain, and triggered anxiety year after year in the wealthiest country in the world. Our government has a military budget equal to the next ten countries' military budgets combined, and the lowest tax rates on large corporations and the superrich in the Western world.

The more you know and the more steamed you become, the more your sense of self-respect kicks in and causes you to stand up and speak out for a more organized labor force, unionized or not. My law school classmate Paul Tobias realized soon after graduation that no one was speaking for the great majority of workers who were not members of unions. He started the National Employment Lawyers Association with thousands of lawyers working to improve the lot of defenseless workers. He even started regular publications to address the emerging rights of workers in various states. Look up some NELA lawyers in your geographical area (nela.org).

Getting steamed as a worker, with other workers, can start the rumble from the grassroots that politicians and their paymasters dread and fear. For they know, deep in the recesses of their monetized minds, that you have on your side morality, fair play, the proper rule of law, and the most fundamental norms of civilized behavior. In a choice between being puny or being powerful behind righteous causes, you'll take up the pursuit of happiness that the latter illuminates. (See my book *Getting Steamed to Overcome Corporatism: Build It Together to Win*.)

CHAPTER THREE

I, the Consumer
Strengthening Economic Democracy

Meeting or greeting people with the usual "Hi, how are you?" is fine, but why not try "Hi, how are your consumer skills today?" You may get a response that is more candid and interesting than the usual "fine" or "I'm good," even if they are not.

Consumer skills are rarely taught in our educational system. Seller skills make up many courses in marketing, advertising, pricing, and accounting, right down to the demands of a credit economy. When people meet in the "free market," this imbalance is overwhelming. There is no contest. Sellers know much more about how to get the shopper or buyer to say yes, especially when the buyer has inadequate information and no time to think.

Consider how much more a car salesperson, insurance agent, home mortgage broker, or payday loan operator knows than the hapless buyer of their products or services. Knowledgeable sellers who are honest enough to resist temptation can help you make a rational choice based on your interest and budget. With sellers who are under the pressure of quotas or sales bonuses or working for a company that has monopoly power—whether a regulated utility monopoly or a company with a monopoly position in a wholesale or retail market (e.g., the only shop around)—the likelihood that you will be fleeced and flummoxed into surrender is not small. In 1970, Senator Philip A. Hart, a Democrat from Michigan and former chairman of the Senate Antitrust Subcommittee, estimated that consumers lost $45 billion yearly because of monopoly pricing. According to the Federal Trade Commission, Americans lost almost $8.8 billion due to fraud alone in 2022.

Vendors getting away with such low-grade practices—which harm the health, safety, and economic well-being of the people— marks an inefficient, wasteful marketplace. Defective products, unanswered consumer calls, denial of health care benefits, and collection agencies rapidly calling to collect debts that often stem from commercial crimes all cause poverty, anxiety, and dread.

The more vulnerable the consumers, the more the corporate classes or corporatists can exert influence and get away with abuses. A more equally advantaged marketplace represents an economic democracy in which both sides, the buyer and the seller, are evenly matched. This is essential for a *political* democracy. Correcting this imbalance has substantial direct and collateral benefits for the environment and the workplace.

My guess is that no more than 10 percent of the population can be described as consistently smart shoppers—people who take time to learn about what they are being offered for purchase and resist immediate gratification. Nutritionally aware consumers reject sugary, fatty, and salty food to improve long-term health and avoid ailments. They may also tap into specialized publications such as *Consumer Reports* or Public Citizen's *Worst Pills, Best Pills* (see worstpills.org). The online subscription allows you to search the *Worst Pills, Best Pills* online database 24-7. Alert consumers are smart about what they want to buy and what not to buy. It also means that what they save from smart shopping is comparable to getting a pay raise. As Ben Franklin used to say: A penny saved is a penny earned.

Astute consumers can also have a beneficial influence on other consumers around them, especially in their household, who ingest, use, or are impacted by what was purchased. Children or elderly people who don't shop still consume. They can benefit or be harmed by the quality of the choices made by those who shop for them.

In this short section, I am not going to run through a checklist for each part of the marketplace to heighten your buying skills. Other authors and I have written many consumer how-to books. Some of these books have become bestsellers, but, alas, are little-used:

- *Winning the Insurance Game: The Complete Consumer's Guide to Saving Money* (1993), by Wesley Smith and me

- *Worst Pills, Best Pills: A Consumer's Guide to Avoiding Drug-Induced Death or Illness* (2005), by Sidney M. Wolfe

- *The Consumer Bible: Completely Revised* (1998), by Mark Green

- *The Frugal Shopper Checklist Book: What You Need to Know to Win in the Marketplace* (1995), by me

- *Buyer Aware: Harnessing Our Consumer Power for a Safe, Fair, and Transparent Marketplace* (2022), by Marta Tellado

People like us are called consumer advocates. We don't like to admit that there is a great gap, for instance, between buying books on how to smartly buy a car or home; how to select a doctor, lawyer, mechanic, or plumber; how to patronize the best financial adviser; and so on, and having shoppers apply this know-how. Even if it is easy to do so and see the immediate benefits, such as dollars saved, safer medicines, or reliable services, many impatient consumers resist learning how to avoid marketplace traps.

There is just too much interference by marketeers and advertisers using trickery to sell charm, glamour, or passion at the points of sale—including pressures to quickly make up your mind. Consumers need to interrupt and say, "Slow down, I've got to think about this purchase and may get back to you."

Therefore, I'm asking you to set aside the handbooks, the manuals—if you indeed have them—and let me encourage you to develop a greater awareness of the significance of your role in the overall economy, which might induce you to develop specific skills for yourself.

It is, as you must know, hard to organize consumers. It has taken the premier consumer-testing organization Consumer Reports almost a century to reach five million print and online subscribers to their eminently useful, low-priced monthly magazine. One would expect many more subscribers in a country of 275 million shoppers! *Consumer Reports* magazine provides reliability ratings, checks for recalls, and tracks maintenance for the name-brand products they review. And now there are competing services such as Wirecutter, owned by the *New York Times*, that provide a similar type of guidance for a younger crowd.

Sometimes consumers unconsciously or intelligently buy or reject products and throw large sellers back on their heels. Some forty million people decided over a period of twenty years in the seventies and eighties that they wanted nutritious food instead of the harmful junk-food diet they were encouraged by print and broadcast advertisers to indulge in. Presto, supermarkets started to provide more healthy foods, helped by mandatory labeling laws. Whole grains, more fresh fruits and vegetables instead of canned foods, and more Mediterranean foods low in fat, sugar, and salt began to fill store shelves. Boutique shops and restaurants offering nutritious food started opening.

When I was little, grocery stores sold soft, bleached Tip Top and Wonder Bread (about which my skeptical mother used to say,

"You know you've picked up these breads without looking at them because your fingers and thumb collide.") Now there is a wide variety of breads worthy of the name. Why? Intelligent consumer demand, spearheaded by vigorous consumer-advocacy groups, such as the Center for Science in the Public Interest, changed the food and nutrition scene (see store.nutritionaction.com).

That's the first step in the elevation of one's consumer significance. With the awareness that you are participating in a stream of signals, you can talk up your preferences to your circle of relatives, friends, and coworkers and register your preferences by telling vendors what you want and urging them to tell their bosses.

This gets you on your way to being a grassroots influencer, unlike the corporate-paid influencers for hire who spread the companies' sales pitches. I once knew a self-made influencer who would go into stores, examine merchandise, and then tell the salesperson exactly why he refused to make a purchase. He would do this to give feedback instead of silently shaking his head and heading for the exit.

Embracing your new role as a self-respecting consumer and shopper is always a wonderful work in progress. It means refining a special character and personality as a purchaser and user of goods and services. For example, if you want to buy a house or rent an apartment these days, the seller, broker, or both will expect you to have a credit score or a credit rating. Insurance companies might set premiums based on your credit record. If you just buy with cash, checks, or money orders and don't have a privacy-invading credit or debit card with all the charges and fine-print baggage, many companies refuse to deal with you. Do you just go away? Or do you object and complain to the authorities about this discrimination and pressure on you to enter the credit-economy gulag, lose control of your money, and be penalized, fined, and overcharged with inscrutable billing codes? By the way, several states prohibit vendors from not accepting cash and more are considering such laws to protect buyers using cash and checks.

Complaining is an invigorating art, and it takes different talents depending on if you are directing your complaints to the vendors or their supposed regulators; members of your state legislature; the US Congress; the consumer reporter at your local newspaper or radio or television station; or as a plaintiff in small-claims court. Remember, in small-claims court, you don't need a lawyer to bring a suit against a cheating vendor.

Speaking of complaints, people always ask: to whom do we go for help? The usual suspects—the state attorney general, the Better Business Bureau, various federal agencies—are often not responsive. But the nearby small-claims courts underused by consumers may be just what you need—they are accessible, you don't need a lawyer, and you get a quick decision. Sometimes the mere mention of filing a small-claims complaint leads the offending seller to settle.

Guiding consumers toward greater awareness of their well-being starts with a conversation, just like all social justice movements do. You can talk about the old days when buyers bargained over price and quantity—say at the food markets or for a doctor's care. "Will you take a couple dozen eggs, Dr. Jones? Because I don't have money to pay you."

Now it is almost totally take-it-or-leave-it price domination by sellers—even small sellers. This rigidity against bargaining comes from the millions of franchised small businesses whose prices and portion controls are a command performance from national headquarters. It also comes from so-called regulated industries who say they are "just following orders" from the regulators they control. It used to be that you could indirectly bargain with your utility by using less of its electricity, gas, water, or telephone services. You used to pay for what you used. No more. These monopolies have developed a formula whereby you pay a certain substantial amount regardless of use. Or, in the case of California for instance, they will increase water rates after asking consumers to cut down on usage in order to make up the difference caused by, say, a drought. The water utility will demand a rate increase from the California Public Utilities Commission (CPUC) to make up the difference.

Showing how in many instances the consumers of yesteryear had more bargaining power gives today's consumers something to think about in their marketplace dealings. "Can you sweeten the proposed arrangement a bit?" might be a regular ask of vendors who have some wiggle room. When numerous consumers show they aren't pushovers, it will give pause to sellers trying to slip something past their customers in general.

My dad, who owned a restaurant/bakery/delicatessen in a small town, would urge his customers to buy local from family-owned businesses whenever they could, pointing to the many advantages, such as the charitable giving of local businesses, which in turn financially support the daily reporting by local newspapers, better customer service at the point of sale, and not being vulnerable to the CEO in some giant corporate headquarters pulling the plug on the local agent or franchisee. He practiced what he preached.

Today, stressing local economic self-reliance is more important than ever for stability, fairness, and creativity. Local renewable energy, credit unions, food cooperatives, community clinics, media outlets, and family-owned industries all circulate money within the community and are likely to be more reachable, helpful, and accountable than the "press one, press two" anonymous voicemail elusiveness of algorithm-driven big business, such as the big banks. Bank of America somehow finds it hard to return telephone calls. An enormous amount of a consumer's time is spent just trying to get through to giant sellers for answers to questions or to resolve complaints. Many give up trying, so the seller wins. Consumers should consider billing giant corporations for unreasonable waiting time.

I was amazed at what is being created by local economies after discovering *YES!* magazine, which likes to report what innovative local businesses or nonprofits are doing all over the country. The Institute for Local Self-Reliance is a research and advocacy organization that has been a leader in decentralizing economic power and building a fight against corporate control of local communities.

Backyard vegetable gardens have proven their worth—you grow fresh fruits and vegetables, get physical exercise close to nature, learn about the food cycle, and can compare flavor to packaged, store-bought produce that endures thousands of miles of travel from the fields where it was grown. There is no lack of helpful manuals. There are even books on ethnic gardens for specialty foods. While not everyone has access to a backyard, there are often community gardens or neighbors who will allow public access to their property or land for a share of the produce. My hometown had a "town farm" for residents to use.

The price of convenience for shoppers is indeed a good topic for conversation—they pay more and get less. I've visited friends in warm climes where grapefruit, lemon, and peach trees abounded in their backyards. Their fruits dropped to the ground uneaten as the homeowners patronized giant food chains for the same fruit. It is truly remarkable how much food can be harvested on a small plot of land.

Vegetable gardens are an invaluable experience for today's sedentary, screen-seduced children to escape the internet gulag and engage in the process of connecting fertile dirt to seeds, water, and sunlight. Teaching children to grow their own food or make their own goods is a great way to make their elementary education mean something for their future. My sister Laura encouraged her children to make their own gifts for their friends or each other's birthdays.

For millennia, people had to produce, hunt, or fish to eat. They made their clothing out of animal skins and plant material. They bartered long before the advent of fungible money. Then specialization by artisans started splitting the role of production from consumption. People made and did things for other people in return for various forms of compensation—producer to consumer. Specialization in the industrial age never stopped becoming ever more intricate and remote from consumers. Now specialization has reached a point where small parts manufactured in Japan supply the entire auto industry. Imagine, 90 percent of all the latest superchips used in the world are manufactured in Taiwan. A break in the global supply chain reverberates around the world, stopping production and raising prices for consumers. But a similar reverberation can reverse the course, with consumer rejection of the final product going up the supply chain to its origins. For example, when people stopped using plastic bags for shopping in favor of reusable cloth or paper bags, their action reverberated all the way to specialty chemical firms supplying raw materials to the plastic-bag manufacturers.

In the internet age, it is possible for such rejections to go viral. This happened when a young woman, Molly Katchpole, saw that Bank of America was going to add another monthly charge to low-volume accounts. She sharply resisted and expressed her indignation online, which drew thousands of Bank of America customer demands against such a charge. Bank of America backed off.

A regular airline passenger, Kate Hanni, found herself and fellow passengers parked on the tarmac in Austin, Texas, for nine hours. Outraged, she spoke out against the weak regulations by the Federal Aviation Administration that had allowed such an isolating incident to occur without a penalty. The public reaction was such that she received lots of mass media publicity, which she converted into a new consumer group called FlyersRights.

I share the above examples to give you a taste of how many levels of engagement are available to you, well beyond your shopping cart or inscrutable utility or hospital bill. Speaking of the latter, computerized billing fraud and abuses in the health care industry itself account for at least 10 percent of all health care costs. Get ready—that is about $360 billion in the year 2023 alone. Less than 1 percent is returned to the fleeced by grossly understaffed federal law enforcement officials. Now, you may say, what is my evidence for this assertion? Always ask this question when you hear figures or estimates. My sources are a General Accounting Office (now the US Government Accountability Office) report, media exposés, and the nation's leading expert on this subject, Harvard University professor Malcolm Sparrow, who says that is a rock-bottom estimate.

The causes of much consumer harm are latent; in other words, hidden or concealed. Probably the most horrific example is that at least five thousand people a week die in US hospitals from "preventable problems." Who says so, you ask? A 2015 Johns Hopkins School of Medicine study—peer-reviewed—in which the authors, who are also physicians, said that this was the most conservative estimate of preventable deaths. What kinds of problems, you ask? Well, hospital-induced infections, neglect during a code blue, wrong combinations of drug prescriptions, understaffing, lack of skill or expected knowledge, and plain old incompetence. (There have been other medical school studies pointing toward such enormous casualty levels.)

Skepticism is a healthy consumer habit. Many products, from meat to medication, do not state their country of origin. Shoppers used to be given that information, but corporate lobbyists got their toady members of Congress to eliminate the requirement for such labels. Over the years, as a result, Americans never learned that there are no more antibiotics manufactured in the United States. Antibiotics!

Skepticism is ripe when you see labels that voluntarily set expiration dates. Studies show these are often set too early to get you to reject the remainder of the package or bottle or speed up its consumption. Both lead to more purchases. Expiration dates are not for decay but for possible slight declines in flavor or taste—almost unnoticeable for several months after the expiration date. They are not safety expiration dates. I once bought rubbing alcohol with 90 percent alcohol. Even this product had a three-year expiration date. When I told my friend Dr. Sidney Wolfe about this, he wryly responded: "Just what does alcohol expire into?"

Too many people take consumer protection for granted and avoid requests to contribute to the small budgets of consumer groups. This affected the aforementioned Kate Hanni of FlyersRights. She fought for airline passengers again and again, with some success, as her financial contributions withered away. Exhausted and working out of a spare bedroom in her California home, she finally quit. Luckily, FlyersRights.org was rescued by Paul Hudson, the father of a sixteen-year-old girl killed in the Pan Am Lockerbie explosion over Scotland on December 21, 1988. Hudson has been an advocate for airline safety for over thirty years and has been the president of FlyersRights.org since 2013. This effective but too-small group operates a shoe-string budget. Airline passengers are taken by what consumer writers have called the "Let George do it" syndrome, meaning: Sure, I'd love to help, but don't worry, someone else will always donate to the group's budgets while I put aside requests for donations.

As a reverberating consumer, you have accepted the routine mission of speaking up and speaking out and, when needed, standing up to abuses and other seller shenanigans. When consumers voice their concerns, they help stop the crooks from driving out honest businesses.

Pollsters call plenty of people. Many call recipients choose not to cooperate and hang up when pollsters contact them. I recommend that you answer consumer polls. Each person in a 1,500-person poll is seen as representing millions of people with similar opinions. That's who you are representing in statistically designed representative professional polls. Knowing how important this role is, when called, jump on it. Polls make the news far more than good reports of solid consumer groups do. The same is true for political polls. Ask the caller why there are almost no consumer issues polled by politicians or political parties. When answering a poll that wants your opinion on certain products or services or certain policies affecting the marketplace, you can ask the pollster why there is rarely a question asking what people think about tougher enforcement and prosecution of corporate crime. Chances are your point may find its way back to those who develop poll questions. Or you can call up the polling firms directly. Anyhow, you are doing your bit and hoping others will do likewise until a question on the corporate crime wave emerges from some polling report. When politicians see the overwhelming conservative/liberal convergence on getting crime out of the suites, it could encourage candidates to campaign on changing corporate criminal law.

You may be part of the majority in this country with adequate health insurance, however pricey. But at least eighty million Americans have either no health insurance or very inadequate coverage. An average of two thousand people a week die because they can't afford insurance to get diagnosed or treated in time (including having regular checkups and, periodically, tests such as colonoscopies). Many more people experience worsened injuries and illnesses for the same reason. So you've got your insurance, why should you be concerned about them? First, as Canadians say, for the sake of social morality and solidarity. Helping each other is what makes a society come closer to the good life for all. Second, for your own safety. Untreated infections can lead to contagion; a virus can pass to you from people you've never heard of but have come into contact with in the normal course of interacting with people in public places such as stores, offices, planes, buses, and trains.

Here's another thought—most people know that restaurant workers are usually low-paid and receive poor benefits with no paid sick leave. You know what I'm going to say next. They go to work sick, and in the restaurant's kitchen or en route to your table they may emit little droplets containing bacteria or viruses that fill the air in closed spaces. Public health workers can infect patients in the same way for the same reason in hospitals and clinics. Paid sick leave and paid family leave are provided in most Western countries, complementing their universal health insurance guarantees. What's our excuse in the "land of the free, home of the brave"? Answer: not enough people speak up as consumers for their own protection to produce the powerful rumble of a mass approaching Capitol Hill. Politicians fear unorganized rumbles from the people, who get louder and louder and are made up of all kinds of political backgrounds. President Richard Nixon signed proconsumer, proenvironment, and proworker legislation between 1969 and 1974 because he heard the rumble from the people coming out of the sixties and early seventies. The Democratic Congress responded to grassroots calls for action.

Did you know you have specialized consumer experts in your community? They are the plumbers, electricians, carpenters, insurance agents, painters, roofers, and interior decorators. They know what you need to know. They know and can tell you which of the products you need are the best, longest lasting, and safest, with good warranties. Tradespeople know about furnaces, boilers, appliances, lighting fixtures, toilets, tubs, paint, plaster, and other household items. These artisans are too infrequently asked for their knowledgeable opinion ahead of choosing their services over those of their competitors.

If you become discouraged by how long your impulsive-shopper friends take to accept your advice, consider having a "fun" conversation that gets them thinking without getting their hackles up. Instead of friendly nudging, try this reverse psychology:

"Hey, buddy, I've figured out ten ways that I can shaft myself as a shopper. Wanna hear them?" "Sure, give it a try." "OK, here goes . . ."

Buy before I think
Buy before I read
Buy before I ask any questions
Buy before I can afford to buy
Buy before I see through the seller's smile and smooth
    pitch
Buy before I comparison-shop
Buy when I am tired or hungry
Buy when I am rushed
Buy to dote on my children or because my kid demands
    the product
Buy just to keep up with my friends or neighbors

Watch their reaction as the humor sinks into a sense of greater self-awareness. Add your own examples of similar one-liners.

After some time developing your skills as an "influencer," you may decide to go to the next level of collective impact. You can join with others to organize a food cooperative or, if you're fortunate to live in a community with an ongoing food co-op, consider joining it and other co-ops such as a daycare co-op or a repair co-op. The National Cooperative Bank was created by Congress in 1978. The bank says, "NCB has an uncommon mandate to ensure our efforts benefit those most in need, supporting low-income communities and the expansion of cooperative initiatives. With this guiding principle, we contribute to the building blocks of sustainable communities: investing in clean energy, small businesses and affordable housing, expanding access to healthy food and affordable health care, plus much more."

Check it out the next time you are in Washington, D.C., or by visiting www.ncb.coop.

Short of co-ops, there are buying clubs online where buyers pool their dollars to negotiate a better deal. This can be done locally or for national products. Beware of large group buying associations, such as the American Automobile Association and the American Association of Retired Persons, which started out claiming they represent numerous consumers then soon went into business for themselves or by privately contracting out to big companies in return for commissions. For example, AARP contracts out its health insurance program to giant UnitedHealthcare and its auto insurance program to the Hartford insurance company, known as The Hartford.

In return, AARP gets commissions and royalties for the use of its well-known name and its referral of members to these vendors. But AARP won't give its own members copies of its contracts with corporations. Over the years, these arrangements help AARP's bureaucracy and bosses more than its members. Some state AAAs went into the auto insurance business, becoming like their corporate counterparts, and cozied up to the auto companies, which they have very rarely criticized for lack of safety, inadequate warranties, overly complicated repairs, poor fuel efficiency, and inadequate pollution control.

There is a more trustworthy alternative to AAA called the Better World Club, which describes itself as "the nation's only environmentally friendly auto club." In addition to offering the traditional services of AAA, such as emergency roadside assistance all over North America for vehicles and bicycles, it pioneers environmentally benign services and advocacy. You can check it out for yourself: betterworldclub.net.

Being a smart consumer is a never-ending journey of discovery, joy, happiness, and self-reliance. Subscribe to the *Nutrition Action* newsletter and receive key reports from the Center for Science in the Public Interest (see cspinet.org). If you or someone you know consumes too much junk food and is overweight, the information from CSPI may spark a healthy transformation in a matter of weeks. The first step toward a healthier body in many observable and out-of-sight internal ways, as with your cardiovascular system, is gaining knowledge. That was the experience of *Washington Post* columnist Colbert King, who wrote about his healthy reversal once he stopped eating fatty, sugary, and salty foods. Good nutrition and exercise further displace the need for commercial products that allegedly meet the needs of a mistreated body. A Mediterranean diet can reduce the need for laxatives that don't work that well and have negative side effects. Less of a red-meat diet lessens the risk of colon cancer and its awful consequences. Many dubious over-the-counter remedies can be replaced by using your shopping know-how.

Of course, the well-publicized self-harm that people inflict on themselves from smoking, taking addictive street drugs or pharmacy-bought drugs, or over-indulging in alcoholic drinks can be diminished or eliminated entirely by a well-honed consumer personality as suggested in this section. Masochistic consumption takes hundreds of thousands of lives a year in the US. It stands to reason that if you are informed and choosy about buying things in the marketplace, you might also be avoiding these addictive immolations or be more predisposed to use your newly acquired shopping acumen to reduce their deadly impact on you and the people who listen to you.

The imbalance of power between buyers and sellers, in favor of the latter, is a manipulation you should take personally. As you take in more details about shopping and consumption, it is motivating to keep in mind how you can take the upper hand away from the driven seller. And keep doing so, with a smile.

CHAPTER FOUR

I, the Taxpayer

The confines of the public discussion about taxes in the US are the narrowest in the Western world. Here corporations and individual taxpayers show concern about the tax rates—income, property, and sales taxes—or how much they are paying in dollars to the federal, state, and local governments. They don't reflect the famous US Supreme Court justice and Civil War veteran Oliver Wendell Holmes Jr., who, when advised by his accountants that he could take advantage of some ways to legally reduce his taxes, retorted that he was not interested, that "taxes are the price we pay for civilization."

There are reasons for this singular focus on taxation levels. Large corporations have figured out how to pay the least amount of taxes by taking advantage of loopholes, lower rates, and foreign tax havens, which allow them to incorporate on remote islands such as the Isle of Man, the Bahamas, or the Cayman Islands. Corporate lobbyists work overtime pushing for unconscionable tax breaks for big businesses. Shirking from paying their fair share, these corporations still demand all sorts of public services and military protections for their investments abroad, plus enormous subsidies, bailouts, and tax holidays paid for by—you guessed it—you, the regular taxpayers. If you are a salaried employee, your taxes are withheld every month. Small-business taxpayers pay up; they don't have high-priced lawyers working for them to contrive intricate tax escapes.

Given this background, it is not surprising that you, the regular, honest taxpayer, don't pay close enough attention to what you're getting or not getting in return for your tax payments. Grumbling about taxes, voting for tax cuts, and even participating in tax revolts are largely the focus of regular taxpayers. There is far less resistance to robust taxes in Western European countries because, unlike the US, their tax revenue comes back to them in universal health insurance, paid university tuition, paid childcare, paid maternity leave, paid sick leave, better public services, and pensions and other public benefits, much of which would make an average American's mouth water. What do you get besides Social Security and Medicare, which you mostly paid for in advance? You pay far more for weapons of mass destruction that could blow up the world many times over. No wonder you grumble—the majority of you elect politicians who promise to cut taxes (mostly, it turns out, for the superrich and big companies). You just want to pay less in taxes. Instead of seeing the benefits of taxes paid returning to your community, you see crumbling roads and bridges, decrepit or nonexistent mass transit, and dilapidated schools and clinics.

Let's say you become more curious about just where your taxes are going, directly and indirectly. You learn that over half of your income taxes goes to the military budget, used to enrich the gouging, massive munitions corporations such as Lockheed Martin, Raytheon, and General Dynamics. These insatiable companies back a sprawling military empire that pursues unconstitutional wars of choice around the world, killing and injuring millions of innocent people whose survivors then hate the United States. Additional amounts of your taxes go to divisions of the government, such as the treasury and agriculture departments. They in turn give away tax credits to rich drug, tech, and Agribusiness titans These companies receive research and development tax-credits for things these so-called capitalists should be doing anyhow to make a profit. By the way, a tax credit reduces a company's taxable income. It is like a check from the Treasury Department made out to profitable companies such as Intel, Cisco, Apple, Microsoft, Google, Pfizer, Moderna, and Eli Lilly.

To make you feel that you can also reduce your taxes, an entire industry has arisen from firms such as H&R Block and Intuit's TurboTax or from tax lawyers advertising for your business so they can fill out your tax returns and save you money. It has become too complex and time-consuming for many individuals to fill out their own returns. So, these companies and firms tell you, you too can get some peace of mind and play the game of tax avoidance. Indirectly, these soothsayers reduce your indignation level and frustration and lessen your demand for reform of the entire rotten, rigged system. While they may save you a few dollars, this industry obscures the much bigger tax savings given to the big boys and the big corporations. The real solution is for individuals and corporations to fully pay their taxes under a progressive system of taxation.

Endless loopholes often bring the effective federal tax rates for the superwealthy and corporations to single digits or zero. Early in this century, for example, General Electric made $5 billion in US-based profit. GE's select team of lawyers and accountants maneuvered the tax code so that GE not only paid zero federal income tax but also received money back from the US Treasury. Sounds crazy, but the complex tax code that corporate lawyers built, through their influence on Congress and their intricate workings of Internal Revenue Service regulations, have turned manipulation of corporate taxation itself into a profit center. In 2022, forty of some of the largest corporations in the US paid no federal income tax on their huge profits. Apple has so perfected the gaming of world tax systems that a separate Senate hearing, which went nowhere, was devoted to its exploits. No wonder Apple CEO, Tim Cook, got his rubber-stamp board of directors to pay him the equivalent of $833 *a minute*. Prize-winning tax journalist David Cay Johnston says that these big companies can now decide what taxes they want to pay—as well as when and where—as they wish. The IRS, its budget stripped by congressional Republicans until 2022, did not have the funds to hire the skilled auditors to go after them. In October of 2023, House Republicans, who now have a majority in the House of Representatives, proposed cutting the IRS budget by over $14 billion.

Big companies desire complexity in tax laws because they have the lawyers and accountants to help them take advantage of the twists and turns. Small businesses can't afford these legal services. When it comes to tax policy, the Big Boys always have the advantage. The Republicans in Congress, by aiding and abetting the rich and the corporations to evade taxes, are still trying to starve the IRS budget to leave the service unable to hire auditors and lawyers to catch these major tax dodgers.

In the late seventies, I had lunch with the director of the IRS. I said to him that tax specialists told me fewer Americans understand the part of the tax code that covers the insurance industry than those who understand Einstein's theory of relativity. He replied: "I would not be surprised at all." I asked what that means in practice. He said those regulations are unenforceable, adding that there are too few actuarial experts in this field and that most are snapped up by the insurance companies, which in turn keeps the IRS from having the skilled personnel to enforce these arcane rules.

This fact may enrage you, the taxpayer. When these giant companies pay no federal income taxes, that means you are sending more actual dollars, as an individual, to Uncle Sam than did profitable companies in the early aughts, such as General Electric, and in 2020, such as Nike, Archer Daniels Midland, and Textron. I once asked a self-confessed cynic how he felt about this situation. He replied: "Well, Thomas Jefferson said that government should do for us together what we the people cannot do individually. So

I feel really proud that I'm individually doing more than my share in supporting Jefferson's definition of government." He gave me a sly wink.

Of course it really is not funny at all. Whenever the superrich and giant corporations get away with paying far less than a progressive system would require them to do—either by lobbying for loopholes or by outright illegal tax evasion—one or more of three things happens. Either you, the taxpayer, pay more taxes, or you and others receive fewer public services, or your children inherit and have to shoulder a bigger deficit. That's the message that's been conveyed for decades by Robert McIntyre, the former director of Citizens for Tax Justice, who would list which corporations paid the least taxes, year after year.

We once had a small Tax Reform Group in the seventies and eighties that exposed tax breaks inserted at the last minute into legislation at the end of a congressional session. We gave our findings to the *New York Times* and *Washington Post* reporters; once they were exposed and stirring up public outrage, the toady lawmakers who sponsored the tax breaks in return for campaign cash often quickly withdrew them. Today, there are fewer full-time, full speed ahead citizen tax watchdogs. That is how weak our civic advocacy community is, and that is where you come in, along with millions of other regular taxpayers.

You can start by looking around. You learn that tricky underpayment of taxes has more than a monetary impact and is unfair to many law-abiding taxpayers. Income tax provides the most perverse incentives you can imagine. For example, half the cost of business lunches involving lots of alcohol and cigars can be deducted as an ordinary and necessary business expense, along with other extravagances so off the moral wall as to not be mentioned in polite company. In 2021 and 2022, businesses could deduct the full cost of work-related food and beverages purchased from a restaurant.

Yet parents can't deduct the amount they pay for disposable diapers or diaper services that launder cloth diaper or maternity clothes.

Now, if you are getting mad and frustrated as hell, that is a good thing. Controlled indignation—often described as a fire in the belly—backed by the facts becomes the engine of action and change. Many experts, years ago, knew all about dangerously designed cars and drunk drivers but didn't move to reduce these perils. It took people who had lost relatives or friends—due to unstable vehicles, drunk drivers, or lack of seat belts—to get safer practices and mandatory lifesaving laws enacted.

These wildest incentives keep you looking for more. You come upon rip-offs: the fact that honest labor is taxed but not toxic pollution or crimes by big business against innocent people. On a trip to Canada, I heard some people calling for tax reform by saying, "Tax what we burn, not what we earn." I added another line: "Tax what we bet, not what we net" (meaning interest on our savings). This was regarding the absence of any sales taxes on gigantic amounts of money speculated on Wall Street, while there is a hefty sales tax of 6 to 8 percent on many of our store or online purchases of life's necessities. A mere 1 percent tax on all stock, bond, and derivative sales would produce about a trillion dollars a year and fall principally on high-income investors and speculators—a special kind of progressive sales tax.

Your curiosity keeps piquing, so you continue your exploration. You stumble on an oft-repeated comment by one of the richest men in the world, Warren Buffett. He has said repeatedly that he pays a lower rate of taxation than his secretary. That is because he can and does take advantage of the tax code in ways she cannot. He thinks this is at odds with what he has long supported—a real progressive tax law that taxes people at higher rates the more they make. Once, he carried this message to a meeting with a group of liberal Democratic senators in Congress. He made his case, as he has done in several op-eds in major newspapers such as the *New York Times*. The senators listened as they munched on their lunch, smiled, thanked him for the meeting, and drifted away. No commitments. No nothing. He was dismayed. Unfortunately, the tone of his voice during our telephone conversation indicated he was so dismayed that he was not going to ask for any more such meetings.

However, Buffett did join an amazingly determined group of some thousand rich people who mobilized pressure to block George W. Bush and Dick Cheney from marshaling enough support in Congress to abolish the federal estate tax entirely. The GOP had been laying the groundwork to allow the wealthy to pass down untaxed estates to their descendants, perpetuating unlimited family dynasties. Political consultant and wordsmith Frank Luntz encouraged the Republican Party to rename the estate tax the "death tax." Led by Chuck Collins and William Gates Sr. (Bill Gates's father), a coalition of concerned rich folks blocked the effort totally. It was a very close vote. The Patriotic Millionaires say, "The estate tax plays an important role in leveling the playing field, improving life for all Americans." Visit patrioticmillionaires.org and you will be surprised by how many progressive economic positions this group supports.

You read this and say to yourself, "Hmm, maybe regular taxpayers have some wealthy allies here." In reading about this battle among the superwealthy, you come upon an assertion by then-president Ronald Reagan, who believed capital gains (from stocks or property) should be taxed at the same top rate as regular income by workers such as yourself. The "Gipper" didn't succeed. Capital gains are taxed at the maximum rate of 21 percent (and often less) compared to the maximum of 37 percent for individual income. To Reagan, income was income, regardless of where it came from. Sounds reasonable, you think.

It suddenly occurs to you that this privileged difference (since most capital gains are incurred by wealthier people) amounts in effect to unequal protection of the law.

Pursuing this contradiction between fairness and power plays on Capitol Hill, you may discover that you are in a congressional district or state whose lawmakers sit on the tax-writing House Ways and Means Committee and the Senate Finance Committee. These are powerful committees indeed, and no one knows this better than the big corporate tax-escape lobbyists swarming the congressional corridors.

Let me offer one case in point. Western Massachusetts is one of the most liberal and progressive areas of the country. Unfortunately, it is represented by Richard Neal, a Democrat who on tax policy acts like a corporate-indentured Republican. After the Democrats won the House in 2018, he became chairman of the House Ways and Means Committee. The first thing he said in January 2019 was that he wasn't going to push for the repeal of the huge Trump tax cuts of 2017 for the rich and powerful or even allow any of his colleagues' subcommittees, such as the one headed by former Texas Supreme Court justice Lloyd Doggett, to have public hearings on Trump's tax giveaways.

Some of his voters objected and asked each other, "What gives here?" The answer comes easily. Just look at his big campaign donors. Disgusted, about 150 of his constituents, helped by an active local librarian, petitioned Chairman Neal to do what he intensely disliked doing—going back home to attend a town meeting to respond to questions of people from this heavily Democratic congressional district. They had a petition delivered to his Washington and Springfield offices, held an informative demonstration in front of his Springfield office, made numerous telephone calls and wrote emails, and fielded vague promises by his staff—all to no avail. Neal wore them out, with the help of pro-Neal newspapers that declined to report on this civic effort, which reflected the majority opinion in his district.

In the "I, the Citizen" chapter, I describe more detailed steps to keep the pressure on recalcitrant lawmakers. The point is that many areas of the country have more leverage on Congress because they are in districts or states with legislators on congressional tax-writing committees. A social media network of your fellow citizens in these districts would speak with a larger bullhorn than individual efforts. Legislators fear such movements, especially when liberals and conservatives work together and display dynamic expansion month after month. It is harder to brush off and delay—much less succeed in gaming—cohesive right–left coalitions.

This networking is essentially what Grover Norquist does. He is the notorious lobbyist who for many years got GOP legislators in Congress to sign his pledge never to raise taxes. The Americans for Tax Reform website shows 42 members of the Senate have signed the pledge, and 189 House members signed on this year. Before the 2012 elections, 242 House members and 41 senators signed on. He backs up his demand with a small, lean, and mean group of constituents back in their districts. ATR is really not that large, probably comprising at most a few thousand followers in the districts and states and a loose network of less driven but like-minded lobby groups in Washington, D.C. A report from Open Secrets says ATR, backed by corporations, spent $4.1 million on political advertising in 2011, and according to the Center for Responsive politics, ATR spent more than $750,000 annually on lobbying. Norquist has been quoted as saying, "I don't want to abolish government. I simply want to reduce it to the size where I can drag it into the bathroom and drown it in the bathtub." Norquist wants a smaller federal government to make it easier to reduce taxes. He gets quite a bit of media, though no reporters ask how his demand for tiny taxes squares with his support of a giant military budget and his opposition to adequate tax revenue for the public works and services that get him and his followers safely to work and home and play. Norquist's lesson is that nothing beats single-minded determination that is laser-focused on members of Congress, appealing to the greed and narcissism of the ruling classes. Norquist doesn't bother with marches and demonstrations—he just works on *in-person* lobbying, Republican by Republican, in Congress. That's why they fear and submit.

You now know enough to read some popular articles and books about real tax reform, and to learn about which people and groups are working to diminish the unfairness of the present "disgrace to the human race," as President Jimmy Carter called the homogenous tax code. You look up some of the groups, such as Citizens for Tax Justice. Good Jobs First deals with the giveaways to companies such as Intel, Amazon, and Walmart that make local governments bid to get their new installations built within their boundaries, in return for years of exemptions on property tax and other local tax. In 1979, our Public Interest Research Group (PIRG) published a report titled "State Competition: Bidding for Business: Corporate Auctions and the Fifty Disunited States," which explained how states try to woo corporate investment by offering tax-free bonds to affluent corporations. All too often, the report found, the companies did not truly need the money and did not, in fact, make decisions about plant locations or expansions based on the subsidies. They just took whatever they could get away with.

You learn how the tax watchdog groups are dealing with Congress and state legislatures. These groups have upgraded their ability to get the attention of these lawmakers. For example, a coalition of environmental groups and consumer groups working with Taxpayers for Common Sense regularly publishes the Green Scissors report to highlight wasteful and environmentally harmful federal spending (see greenscissors.com). The Patriotic Millionaires say they want a tax system that "prioritizes the interests of working people over the wealthy and works to constrain democracy-destabilizing levels of inequality."

Their three tax priorities are:

1. Tax all income over $1 million in the same manner, regardless of how it was generated;
2. Implement a truly progressive federal income tax by making changes at both the top and bottom; and
3. Institute a wealth tax that constrains extreme wealth concentration.

For more information, see: patrioticmillionaires.org.

I can't tell you how many times members of Congress who want to do the right thing say to us that they hardly hear from anybody back home complaining about tax policies other than to ask for the reduction of their own taxes. One congressman, Charles Vanik, from Ohio, used to put out a widely publicized list of large companies shirking tax obligations every year, yet still did not get the kinds of letters and calls to his colleagues needed to move them to support his reform legislation. There is no district-by-district citizen lobby for tax fairness.

Now we've reached the stage where it is up to you as to how far you want to go in time and effort to join or build grassroots heat. You could become a sturdy, smart, outspoken taxpayer, writing a letter to the editor or op-ed or calling in to a radio talk show. You could be a conversationalist on tax topics with your friends, relatives, coworkers, or any students in your circle. After all, justice movements tend to start by replacing some daily small talk with significant talk about societal betterment—just the way our forebears did before 1775 in the thirteen colonies. You might call reporters suggesting any number of timely stories, especially around April 15—Tax Day. Or call a local high school principal to tell them about a retired corporate tax lawyer, John Fox, who developed a high school course on taxes that worked. The kids got it.

You might ask your town or city council to arrange a public meeting on tax reform and simplification, with invitations to your senators and representatives and state legislators. That's an idea that might catch on in your community. During the election season, you may send a letter asking the candidates to tell you and your friends where they stand on issues *a*, *b*, *c*, *d*, etc. By this time, you may have started a small, informal group of fellow citizens with a nice letterhead to convey that you are not speaking as a loner but are riding a ripple that could turn into a wave. Normally, smug lawmakers begin to change when they see a movement arising out of their apathetic constituents. Members of Congress start talking about the agitation and rumble from the people, among themselves in committee rooms, at lunch, or in chance meetings in the corridors. I've seen such heightened lawmaker concern about the arising masses firsthand. In the back of the most corporatized legislator's mind is the fear that "the pitchforks are coming," as the metaphor goes. For they know how pressed and exploited honest people are daily as well as you do, maybe more because they see the anxiety, dread, and fear of the families they encounter during their routine visits around their congressional district and state.

Make civic initiatives part of your daily rhythms and keep in mind the element of serendipity—defined as "finding valuable or agreeable things not sought out." A benefactor, an ally, an academic expert, or a lawmaker may well emerge that you never expected to show up in person or on your screen. Someone who knows about mass mailing or crowdsourcing may sizably expand your circle, your group. That may lead to getting a growing number of lawmakers on your side. Public hearings and media coverage may converge. Others like you around the country may take heart and duplicate your efforts. When the time is ripe, large numbers of previously passive, fed-up people will start supporting your efforts to build a forceful civic movement.

In states and localities where there are referenda—people voting their own laws into reality—tax revolts spread widely. One example is California's Proposition 13, in 1978, to limit property taxes to 1 percent of the full cash value of a property, and to limit increases in property valuation to 2 percent per year. Prop 13 was launched by two men, Howard Jarvis and Paul Gann, who unleashed a thunderbolt that shocked the country and made them celebrities. Unfortunately, this "reform" also froze money for school systems and over time favored the homes owned by older people and discriminated against the unprotected homes bought by younger people after the referendum's cutoff date. Beware of how such referenda can backfire over time.

Note that the same tool of direct democracy can be used to flatten out the unfairness at the state level that rewards the upper-income classes and corporations with tax breaks at the expense of the lower-income taxpayers and the needed public services that go begging. As you may be expanding your goals, keep the referendum in mind for both prudently reforming tax rates and controlling the uses of tax revenues.

Before you feel the usual tug of being a drop in the ocean, remember the parable of the rivulets that are the source of the mighty Mississippi River, mentioned in the "I, the Citizen" chapter. Do not accept without rebuttal any arguments that taxes are too complex for people to understand and act upon. Years ago, Public Citizen's Tax Research Group published *People and Taxes*, a newspaper that repudiated such cries of despair, and a book titled *Tax Politics: How They Make You Pay and What You Can Do About It* (1976). Besides, any part of the tax code that is too abstruse should be subject to plain-English regulations that expose the uses of complexity, or what Thomas Paine called "mysteries," to mask serious evasions and enforcement of the tax laws. That is why taxpayers like you are so critical to the rise of forces for change— you must pursue clarity to understand where you wish to go. You become part of the people's lobby for clarity and the abolition of gobbledygook as a tactic by the exploiters of the present legalized insanity of outright criminal tax evasion.

Remember to master some details of the corporate and super-rich methods of not paying taxes. Three books by prizewinning *New York Times* reporter David Cay Johnston, who now writes and teaches at Syracuse Law School, will put you in the top 1 percent of the citizenry for arguing your case. (See the Resources for Action appendix for the titles.) They are superb writings of clarity whose works you can use to impress your members of Congress and the media.

CHAPTER FIVE

I, the Voter

Ever hear of the expressions the "smart voter" or the "conscious voter"? Probably not. Most voters, alas, are anything but. There are ideological voters, impulsively emotional voters, one-issue voters, voters who align with a party based on their shared ethnic background, voters who align with the party favored by the previous generations of their families, gender voters, race voters, geographical voters, and mad-as-hell voters. All these voters set themselves up for manipulation and control by pandering politicians who have uncanny antennae on how best to flatter, fool, and flummox them. If you're in any of these voter categories, you may be in sync with a slice of the candidate you voted for, but you'll be on the losing end of the politician's performance and agenda once they're elected.

Let's face it, politicians spend a lot more time figuring out how to sell themselves to you than you do figuring out how you can wisely say "no sale." To be sure, voters are deprived of having more than just two choices on the ballot aside from the Republican and Democratic duopoly that often backs the same corporate interests. This limits your voter bargaining power compared with a country in which one has more political choices, voices, and parties working to earn votes, which enhances a democracy.

Still, the smart voter demands more choices of agendas and candidates. Publicizing this demand will improve their chances of getting more and better candidates and agendas on the ballot.

Also, it will make it more likely that state laws obstructing who gets on the ballot (the highest hurdles in the Western world) will become less prohibitive.

There are two principles that smart voters should consider. First, once elected, any candidate will be a trustee with the authority you have given them under the Constitution. That is why the US is called a republic. Our Constitution's preamble starts with "We the People," not "We the Congress" or "We the state legislature." The voter possesses the sovereign power. Elections are to delegate this sovereign power to whomever gets the most votes (except for the anti-democratic Electoral College's role in presidential elections). So, voters should take seriously the misuse of their delegated power, rather than cavalierly persist in saying out loud "I'm not into politics," "I don't care about politics," or "Politics doesn't mean anything to me." No matter how hard you try, you cannot escape "politics," because in a myriad of different ways, politics is always "into you"!

Second, rotten politics is ultimately a reflection of the disinterest and ignorance of the voters, half or more of whom don't even bother to come out to vote in the November elections and even fewer of whom vote in the primaries. This is an inescapable fact of life in any contemporary society. When such disengagement and ignorance continue for a long time here in America, it plants the seeds in other countries for the establishment of an "elected dictatorship" or worse—a military coup d'état imposing a totalitarian regime without going through phony formalities of a rigged election. This principle is instructed by the ancient Roman lawyer Marcus Cicero's eternal definition of *freedom*. "Freedom," he wrote, "is participation in power." As the more contemporary saying goes, "If you don't demand a seat at the table, you are going to end up on the menu."

Invigorated by these two principles, which should be illustrated and taught to elementary school children, how does one go about becoming a continually smarter and more conscious voter?

Like other endeavors or pursuits in life, it pays to do your homework. This means that you study the record and inaction of the candidates before you weigh the authenticity of their rhetoric, which you can find everywhere from their mass media and social media buys. Unfortunately, politicians get elected primarily on what comes out of their wily mouths, especially since many are in servitude to corporate interests instead of to the people. It is truly amazing how many voters fall prey to candidates' simple words and phrases that validate their impulsive emotions. A recent, devastating example is how Trump, a failed businessman—riddled with bankruptcies, betrayals, deceptions, recurring outright lying, and violations of laws—worked his way through the Electoral College (he lost the popular vote by three million) to the White House on fact-starved speechifying and promises that hit the right emotional buttons, triggering thunderous ovations.

Once you review a candidates' records, make a list of positions that you favor on one side of a sheet of paper. Then flip it over and see how many times the candidates register with your preferences. This becomes, in effect, your own poll of the candidates on matters dear to you, your family, your community, the country, and the world. It leads to building a mandate behind your vote made up of your agenda items, which then get the candidates' attention. Election winners should respect the mandates of their voters. By the way, it is easier than ever to locate the records and voting philosophies of politicians, along with other details, such as whether they favor robust debates with their opponents or whether they dislike letting voters learn how they perform at such focused public events. All kinds of websites make reliable information available to the public for free. (See the Resources for Action section at the back of this book.)

This exercise makes you a multi-issue voter and helps you avoid the vulnerability of being seen by the candidate as just a one- or two-issue voter. The latter voters set themselves up for being dismissed once the candidate answers yes or no. It is also not fair to the candidate, who may be with you on other important reforms, redirections, and civic values. If you judge them over, say, twenty to twenty-five subjects, you are increasing your influence by aggregating your demands into expectation levels for their performance. Candidates are not ready for this kind of voter. Politicians like to run on three or four issues under slogans such as Make America Great Again, Peace Through Strength, or Build Back Better. As they say in football, spread your offense. The more voters do this, the more likely there will be broader media coverage when the candidates begin to discover that the voters can generate high-attention issues. For example, take corporate crime enforcement, which politicians assiduously ignore, for obvious reasons. After all, as a *Business Week* poll discovered in 2000, more than 70 percent of Americans believed that "corporations have too much control over their lives." That's a lot of liberals and conservatives on the same important page. Imagine what they would say today amid a greater corporate crime wave, the staggering disparity in wealth and income between the remote few and the many over whom they rule, and the internet's commercial systems of influence and control. Add massive billing fraud, gouging prices, stagnant real wages, denial of insurance benefits, direct marketing of harmful products to children, anti-unionism by the plutocrats, fine-print contracts favoring sellers in every way, more obstacles toward using the courts, and more corporate control of the public's assets, such as public lands and airwaves. It stands to reason that ever more people—conservatives and liberals alike—feel so unilaterally enchained by the corporate state of Wall Street over Washington.

One way for you to become a smarter voter is to talk about voting with your friends, coworkers, neighbors, and relatives. In a way, it's like a hobby where you become more skilled by discussing it with other hobbyists. Here is a hypothetical you can use:

Suppose a person knocks on your door one Saturday afternoon and says: "Hi, I'm your new neighbor. Just want to let you know I can increase your taxes; send your young men and women to war; let big companies get away with harming your health, safety, and economic well-being; and, by the way, you're helping to pay my salary and all kinds of benefits that you probably don't receive. Thank you for listening. Goodbye!" The person starts walking away from your door. You call out, "Hey there, you mean a lot to me, so I better mean more to you. Come back here. We need to talk some!" Well, that's your member of Congress. If you had a neighbor with that kind of power over you, I don't think you would say: "How dare you interrupt me with politics while I am watching my favorite football team in action." You would instead pay considerable attention to that person and urge others in the neighborhood to do the same.

Haven't you heard cynics blurt out that "all politicians are crooks" or listened to some skeptic declare, "Politicians will tell you what you want to hear and then break their promises after they get elected. That's why I'm not voting." Is there ever any pushback by anyone in the room? It must be a cultural thing for people who make such cavalier dismissals of officeholders, who use *your* power delegated to them, to be viewed as chic or clever. The ancient Greeks in Periclean Athens applied cultural sanctions to people who had no interest or engagement in the community's efforts at betterment. These people were called "idiots" or, roughly translated, "ignorant persons." It is not necessary to use such summary labels. But it would spark a lively and serious discussion to point out that if everyone dropped out of politics, society would fall into dictatorial control, making life insufferable.

Part of the problem is that the cynics and skeptics have difficulty stepping back from their short-circuited aversions and thinking about the kinds of *expectations* they should have for any high political office, apart from those who now occupy the post.

Just ask them to make a list of what they expect from the president of the United States. The office of the president controls many federal departments and agencies with far-ranging power and influence over just about every aspect of your life. Ask your fellow voters to make a list of such topics and issues as war and peace; taxation; protections for children, laborers, and consumers; maintenance of public facilities, the environment, and public lands; access to the media; the courts, government openness, campaign reforms, and recruitment of the best possible civil servants; preparations for how the citizenry should approach pandemics and weather changes; whether candidates set personal examples in language, behavior, honesty, and morals; and, perhaps the most important and least-mentioned expectations, what specific ways do voters want the president to *empower* the citizens in their country to make the ideal of self-government more real.

Developing expectations for the president or any other elected official takes you far out of the superficial responses to what these users of your sovereign power do on any given day. If all you are doing is having knee-jerk reactions to the headlines of a story or a quote by an elected politician, you are being restricted by the narrow and often slanted reporting of the mainstream media. Using the *lever of expectations* helps you generate your own agenda and becomes the yardstick you choose to measure the worth of elected officials. It is a way of empowering you and attracting more of your friends to that level of evaluation. After all, "expectations" are another word for "wishes" (though grounded in an elected official's lawful authority). That leads to questions such as: What if? Why not? How come? By what authority? These sorts of questions are followed by action.

When your expectations, rooted in the politician's proper jurisdiction (e.g., you can't ask a mayor or governor, in their *executive* branch roles, to enact a law without prior legislative action), are presented to your elected representatives, you are providing a novel kind of voter feedback. For example, in a pandemic, a drug company triples the price of the drug that's most needed just to make more profit and cites its monopoly patent for legitimacy. In turn, the federal government, under an existing law, to save lives, can override the patent, set the price, or, if necessary, even produce the drug itself.

During the Vietnam War, the Pentagon started researching and developing its own antimalaria drugs for soldiers. The drug companies had declined to develop these drugs because they were taken so infrequently that they were not deemed profitable. Knowing this history gives voters an expectation and an expanded sense of the kinds of demands they can make to government officials. Too many politicians, including graduates of Harvard and Yale law schools, exploit voters' ignorance and bamboozle them into despair and discouragement.

There are two questions that all voters should keep in mind when interacting with politicians, who are notoriously loose with their facts and the laws. These are:

1. What is the legal authority for your response or declaration?
2. What is the evidence to back up your claim?

These two questions—summarizable as "What's your basis?"—are vital to putting the politicians on the defensive, where they belong if they are in the habit of saying one thing to you while kowtowing to commercial interests in the legislature or to a regulatory agency. How many times have you heard prosecutors throw up their hands and say they don't have the authority to go after x, y, or z corporate criminals? Sure, there may not be a criminal penalty in the law, having been neatly eliminated during its passage by corporate lobbyists, as with the auto and aviation safety laws. But they don't tell you that they have evidence the companies lied to them when answering subpoenas or giving depositions. It is a felony under federal law to lie to the federal government. Again, the more you read, the more you know about new levels of expectations you can hurl against those who are not fulfilling their public trust on behalf of the people.

It is fun and empowering for you and your friends to play the expectations game. Who can contribute the most to a list of expectations, including access to politicians' offices and receptionists, to be sent in a cosigned letter to elected officials or to candidates for public office? Watch the politicians' reactions, including whenever they meet you on the campaign hustings to shake your hand and react to your heightened expectations of them.

In my hometown of Winsted, Connecticut, after flooding of the Mad River destroyed property and cost numerous lives, my mother had had enough with the delay in constructing a simple dry dam to take in heavy loads of water in a flood zone. We were also directly affected: we had lost our entire restaurant/bakery/delicatessen in the great flood of 1955 as a result of Hurricane Diana. The dam should have been built by the Army Corps of Engineers, but they were not responsive to the town's needs. My mother's expectation then shifted to Senator Prescott Bush (R-CT), who was on a campaign trip to our town. She stood in line at the reception until it was her time to shake his hand. She didn't let go of his hand until she expressed the town's desperate need for a dry dam and that only he had the power to make it happen. He answered: "Yes, Mrs. Nader, I'll get it done." And he did. The town hasn't had a Mad River flood since. This is what can happen when voters know enough to shift expectations onto other powers, as to the right officials at the right time.

Another benefit of becoming an expectations pursuer is that it raises the expectations you have for yourself as a voter so you don't just shuffle to the polls to fulfill the minimum civic responsibility of voting. Just "doing your duty" at the polls is important, but safeguarding our democracy requires more. If you find spending some time being a smart voter important and enjoyable, why not form a smart voters club with a letterhead? It can begin with a half dozen friends and develop a specialty of writing compelling letters to legislators. There is a modest skill in how you can write such a letter, including cc'ing important people, reporters, political opponents, and so forth. Soon you will be receiving more responses from your representatives to your letters, emails, and telephone calls. You will stand out in a sea of passive citizenry. Escalating to this club stage will start opening more windows of opportunity—such as writing an op-ed for the local newspaper, receiving calls from the press, or being contacted by frustrated civic groups who want your support. Since you are a citizen volunteer, you can control the time you wish to give to your widening circle of civic engagers. Remember, this is in your role as a voter, so your focus would be on elections and candidates and their policy agendas.

It is always good to read about close elections in which a tiny increase in voter turnout would have sent the better candidate to the legislature, which in turn would have helped tip the balance in that body. It happens. One vote can make a difference. Some elections have ended up in a dead tie or had so close a margin that a get-out-the-vote drive in a neighborhood or two would have made the difference. The Reverend William J. Barber II, who organizes the Poor People's Campaign, has accurately declared that a 10 percent increase in poor people turning out to vote would have given them higher minimum wages, access to health care, and support for their children, among other policies that have long been solidly supported in public-opinion polls but fall short because not enough people go to the only polls that count.

You may wish to expand your hobby by volunteering as a precinct worker on election day. You may so relish your role and engagement in politics that you run for elective office yourself.

In the November 2022 congressional elections in Washington State, Marie Gluesenkamp Perez, who owned a small auto repair shop with her husband, had had enough of the political mess and ran for the seat. She was not at all dissuaded from taking on the much-favored Republican candidate. She won based on authenticity, energy, and plain talk about where she was coming from.

Civic rhetoric is best when it is delivered in plain language that, if challenged, can be backed up by facts. Politicians' speech is too often so carefully scripted that they don't use plain language and think no one notices their lack of authenticity. In fact, voters are very good at seeing through political phonies but vote for them anyhow given limited choices.

In 1948, the Republican governor of New York, Thomas E. Dewey, was viewed as the likely winner of the presidential election. Polls and pundits predicted the defeat of his main opponent, Harry S. Truman. That was before the Truman campaign rented a train and launched a cross-country "whistle-stop" tour. Truman ran against the "do-nothing Congress" and the Republican ties to Wall Street. On September 18, 1948, at the National Plowing Match, in Dexter, Iowa, Truman verbally pummeled the Republican Party and its big-business allies.

Note Truman's plain but powerful language: "I wonder how many times you have to be hit on the head before you find out who's hitting you? . . . These Republican gluttons of privilege are cold men. They are cunning men. . . . They want a return of the Wall Street dictatorship. . . . I'm not asking you to vote for me. Vote for yourselves." Truman had the winning strategy and got 49.6 percent of the vote. Dewey only received 45.1 percent.

Sometimes very rich people make statements that are useful in reaching your friends, neighbors, and coworkers. Here is megabillionaire Warren Buffett from Omaha, Nebraska, who once exclaimed that there is definitely class warfare in America, "but it's my class, the rich class, that's making war, and we're winning."

One of our greatest plain-language populists, Texan Jim Hightower, has delivered pages of usable, repeatable one-liners that are so right on. He has said, "Politics isn't about left versus right; it's about top versus bottom." Hightower knows what the "greedhounds" are doing to all the people in America and that "the corporations don't have to lobby the government anymore. They are the government." For more about Jim Hightower, visit jimhightower.substack.com.

Another type of civic power can be exercised through direct democracy—letting voters change things at or between elections by voting for laws.

The initiative process allows citizens to pass or repeal laws and amend their state's constitution. The referendum process allows citizens to vote to keep or reject a law passed by their state legislature.

The recall process allows citizens to remove an elected official from office. I call this giving elected officials early retirement. This lever of democracy is available to voters in more than twenty-four states and some municipal jurisdictions. Richard Winger's *Ballot Access News* is the best source of information on these direct democracy issues: ballot-access.org.

Barry Klein is one of the most respected property-rights activists in the country. He created the Houston Property Rights Association, back in 1992, to fight flawed zoning laws in Houston. He specializes in mobilizing voters and guiding activist groups of all stripes on how to use direct democracy, especially in the form of charter amendments, to bring political reform at the city level. His civic hobby is alerting people around the country about how little these tools of democracy are used. He shows people, especially at the local level, how they can bring about change in their communities.

You can open so many doors by adding reading to your smartvoter hobby list. It is always remarkable how many people are practicing or showing how to practice the many different muscles of a democratic society but receive little media coverage.

Remember Richard Winger from the "I, the Citizen" chapter? In addition to using direct democracy tools, he knows all about the state ballot-access laws and the ways they restrict voters' choices by blocking third-party or independent candidates. State by state and over and over again, he shows why lower barriers to these candidates allow voters to increase their bargaining power vis-à-vis the two-party duopoly.

Voters taking action to make things better in a democratic society is what a democracy is all about. People are rarely treated well or given anything by the 1 percent and its corporations without demands. Our history is full of illustrations verifying this point. Accordingly, democracy starts with expectations and civic motivation—sharpened by reading, thinking, and conversing. Assuming all that, the final ignition is to have fire in your belly. To say this in a more scholarly way, call it having the emotional intelligence to right what you believe is wrong.

Good luck on your explorations.

CHAPTER SIX

I, the Parent

Modern living has its blessings, but the commercial culture and political economy make it hard for today's parents to fulfill their essential obligations. Consider the pressures on a two-parent household—each parent holding down a job requiring a lengthy daily commute while trying to raise one, two, three, or more young children. For a single parent, the stress is exacerbated. It's rarer than ever for extended family to live nearby, so most parents don't have someone to rely on for help, advice, babysitting, and sharing joy. In its place are commercial services that too often constitute what law professor and parent Edgar Cahn called "the commodification of the family."

Indeed, it is difficult to find any familial role, other than providing love, that is not available for a price. Vendors feast on parents' lack of time—the economic system requires two wage earners just to make ends meet—and use "convenience" as an enticement. From the earliest days of an infant, the aggressive infant-formula business steps in with free formula samples before the mother leaves the hospital. Mother's milk is painted as submodern and inconvenient. In 1998, I, with Gary Ruskin, founded the Commercial Alert project to keep the commercial culture within its sphere and to prevent it from exploiting children and subverting the higher values of family, community, environmental integrity, and democracy. Today, commercialization of society is even more rampant. Home cooking is overshadowed by takeout and fast-food outlets. Commercial childcare, counseling, and recreation have diminished the role of family and community in providing these undertakings. Commercialized sports erode the core ideals, values, and ethics of sports, resulting in escalating incidents of poor sportsmanship and more spectators and fewer participants in athletics. Commercialization of entertainment, public/private education curricula, and health care (replete with overdiagnosis, overmedication, and overcharges) damages our society. All this limitless commercial influence leads to young boys becoming addicted to violent war videos and young girls succumbing to cosmetic marketing. The constant barrage of marketing directly geared to children and parents by commercial sellers is eroding the parent-child relationship and undermining parental judgment. Abi Moore, a cofounder of Pinkstinks, said: "Selling make-up to three-year-olds is sexualising them because the point of make-up is to make yourself more beautiful for someone else to look at you."

The corollary is losing the benefits of the development of parental judgment, which is often being outsourced from families and friends to paid child psychologists or other vendors. Corporate pressures follow children as they grow into their tween and teen years. Tightly clutched smartphones convey corporate-created temptations, seductions, and addictions that digitally abduct children for hours every day. The internet gulag knows no bounds.

Intricate planning by the profiteering, privacy-destroying wardens led by Facebook/Meta/Instagram, YouTube, and TikTok envelop children. The loss of parental control, guidance, and nurturing of children to these electronic child molesters has created an industry worth half a trillion dollars annually. Many studies have shown that direct marketing to youngsters of goods and services that are harmful to their physical and mental health, through smartphones and computers, is relentless. *Who's Raising the Kids? Big Tech, Big Business, and the Lives of Children*, by Susan

Linn documents the damaging corporate influence on children. Marketing by circumventing parents used to be a social taboo. No longer. The links between youngsters and corporatists are secured by smartphones and other technologies using the metaverse and augmented reality. A clear result is that a billion youngsters—no matter the culture or geography—are immersed in an ever more virtual reality separating them from parents, community, nature, or what comprises reality. The drawbacks of growing up in these anxiety-producing technological fantasies are left to perplexed parents to figure out. A report issued by UNICEF titled *The Metaverse, Extended Reality and Children* notes that the "Metaverse and XR-related technologies could pose risks for children's cognitive and social development."

The first step toward teaching your children how to anticipate and confront the realities coming at them is to take control of what is arguably the most important mission in your life. You would willingly give your life to save the lives of your children. So how can you allow that undertaking to be affected by external pressures whose aim is to make a profit first and foremost, regardless of children's well-being? Tobacco, alcohol, deceptively promoted painkillers, junk food and drink, and violent video games are hazardous to your children's health.

Your own parents and grandparents may have suggestions about raising children, but they didn't bring up their offspring in the internet age. Today, corporations are raising your defenseless kids to become knee-jerk customers for what they are selling. Psychology professor Susan Linn details the problem in her 2022 book *Who's Raising the Kids? Big Tech, Big Business, and the Lives of Children.* Unlike with past generations, corporations are your daily competition. Corporations peddle around the clock to your child, in a pipeline that you can't see, for an average of five to six hours a day. They are introducing kids to online gambling and inducing them to nag their parents to buy an endless array of products. The pitches keep getting more odious, insidious, coercive, and reckless. Commercial pornography online is rampant, and little effort is made to keep children from being able to watch it. The advertising industry knows what it is doing to these children because advertisers use words such as "the corporate parent" and "the high nag factor" to describe praiseworthy features of their ads.

Forewarned about these commercial abductions of your children, you can establish practices and routines to shield them, but these can generate rebellious behavior about what to eat, drink, see, and hear because of the pervasive influence of programming created by these "corporate parents." Companies now are using increasingly manipulative algorithms to capture your children's hearts and minds.

As my parents demonstrated, democracy and citizenship start with reading, thinking, and family conversations. Our house was full of books and our daily town newspaper. We listened to the evening news on the radio, which took much longer than today. What can you do today? Some say restrict the use of smartphones at least until kids enter high school. Get them used to looking you in the eye and conversing in ways that spark their innate curiosity, imagination, and intellect. From an early age, as shown repeatedly in the research of Harvard professor Robert Coles, children pick up on the difference between right and wrong. As they reach the age of nine or ten, they become aware that not all is right with the world—dire poverty, rampant hunger, wars, natural disasters, and pollution solutions, such as solar energy, are not applied fast enough. By their tween years, they are full of practical idealism. If, that is, they can be shielded from the wardens of the internet gulag who twist their minds into conditioned responses to ads, increased tolerance for nastiness and hateful speech, and increased disclosure of personal information.

Parents have always had to pay attention to make sure their children do not fall into the wrong crowd of ruckus-prone classmates or neighbors. Nowadays, peer groups are a special focus of the fomenters of direct-marketing madness. Corporations pay teenagers or younger kids to become influencers and promote products to their ever-widening circles of youngsters in person or via social media. These influencers steer their "followers" to buy whatever they are paid to promote. The FTC requires influencers who endorse a product through social media, an endorsement to disclose any "financial, employment, personal, or family relationship with a brand." Nonetheless, in November of 2023, the FTC staff sent letters to a dozen individual influencers and two trad associations "warning them warning them about the lack of adequate disclosures in their Instagram and TikTok posts promoting the safety of the artificial sweetener aspartame or the consumption of sugar-containing products."

As you know from your own recollections, peer groups of youngsters can be cruel, merciless, and relentless. My mother used to interview our new friends while she fed them nice lunches. She would inform us as to why it was necessary at times to "turn your back on the pack." Now it is frequently necessary, in these times of fractured privacies and immodesties, to have parents do that more than ever. Claiming one's independence from peer pressure is a precondition for stable personalities with leadership attitudes and later achievements in the civic community.

The road to becoming civically engaged on the way to civic leadership often starts early. When I asked well-known leaders in contemporary movements for justice how they got started, most of the time the replies involve their parents taking them to rallies, marches, town meetings, and similar public functions, including visiting courts to observe trials. The other explanation speaks to family enlightenment or tragedies due to wrongdoing or criminal neglect, as with dangerous defects in consumer products, avoidable collisions, or toxic exposures in neighborhoods or workplaces.

Our family was no exception. We got started early, with my mother instructing us to be alert to any needs of or emergencies affecting two elderly widows in nearby homes. We also knew my father did not turn down any penniless, hungry person in his restaurant during hard economic times.

Such exposures taught us compassion and charity. As we headed into preteen and teen years, regular family conversations started moving us to think about the differences between charity and justice, and to consider how structural solutions dealing with the root causes of problems can, in the long run, address immediate needs and afflictions. It is useful to foresee and forestall to lessen the need for charity. This includes developing safety devices or enforcing health-and-safety-related government standards or paying livable wages. Our small town of nine thousand people was full of factories and fabrication shops. People got injured. There was little regulation. While helping Dad in the restaurant, I saw workers sitting at the counter with scars or without a finger or thumb, or coughing from dangerous, dusty workplaces. Sometimes they came for coffee, having lost their jobs due to a permanent occupational disability. Workers' compensation paid little for such life-altering injuries or illnesses on the job.

The books in our house were more nonfiction than fiction. These volumes taught us how the cruel exercises of runaway power produced so many avoidable injuries. One by one I read the famous muckraking books by Ida Tarbell on the Standard Oil Monopoly, Lincoln Steffens on urban political and business corruption, and George Seldes on the thousand wealthiest Americans and how they procured such riches on the backs of millions of innocent people. So excited was I by these revelations—never studied in school—that I actually trembled while turning page after page. Upton Sinclair's many short novels, depicting historical truth in personal terms, sometimes brought tears to my eyes.

Clearly the family environment, with mother and father and my older brother and two older sisters, encouraged me to to immerse myself in reading and critical thinking. And the town library, where I borrowed endless numbers of books, three at a time, was two short blocks away.

Plenty of normal fun, play, and laughter kept me from becoming overly obsessed and discouraged by a tormented, war-torn world. We were lucky. Many families had to endure hardships. Some lived in inadequate housing or were food insecure. In some families, parents and children alike had to work multiple jobs to make ends meet. Access to childcare and health care was limited.

Nonetheless, it is noteworthy that so many of the nations' civic leaders on the ramparts for justice came from poor families headed by brave, resourceful parents who "kept their eyes on the prize," as they used to say in the civil rights movement. These parents would connect with their churches, find like-minded people in their children's schools, and constantly strive to pay the family bills.

Young people are often told by adults to focus on getting a good education and wait until they graduate before joining any fray. But being a civic advocate and addressing public controversies is a big part of a good education. Students are not merely citizens-in-waiting. Even my excellent contract-law professor, Lon Fuller, advised law students in their early to midtwenties to hold off on joining the struggles for justice, believing that active involvement in fighting injustices would rupture the concentration and solitude needed for mastering their law school courses.

Too often, young people are advised to not make use of some of the most idealistic years of their lives—years free of crass calculations, such as keeping quiet if you want to be promoted or staying silent because you'll be singled out as "not a team player."

My sister Claire heard these "wait until you're grown up" attitudes while writing her recent book. She thinks it is better to directly address nine- to twelve-year-olds about topics they need to understand if they are to liberate themselves from commercial culture.

While doing research for her book, *You Are Your Own Best Teacher*, she came across many youngsters who had heard, read, and thought about awful conditions in this world and simply resolved they were going to do something about it. They came mostly from humble family backgrounds. They did not have rich or influential parents. But their families gave them a moral compass that pointed them to no-nonsense action or activities. Kids can achieve an awareness and consciousness suitable for their innate curiosity and idealism.

She related the story of Cavanaugh Bell. He pulled together care packages consisting of donated groceries and supplies for the elderly in his hometown of Gaithersburg, Maryland, and filled two semitrucks with food, blankets, jackets, and other essentials for Native Americans on the impoverished Pine Ridge Reservation in South Dakota. Cavanaugh explained how he started his compassionate efforts at age seven: "After I was bullied and felt a darkness inside of me, I knew I didn't want other kids to feel the same way I felt. So I asked my mom if she could help me spread love and positivity. And the more I gave back to my community, the more I wanted to keep doing it." He was helped by people locally and on social media who were taken by his amazing maturity and his determination and sense of urgency to get things done. Donors to his cause understood the urgency of his mission and made timely contributions.

Felix Finkbeiner didn't wait either. In 2007, this nine-year-old German boy was astonished by Wangari Maathai, a Kenyan woman whose life was dedicated to restoring her country's forests. She received the Nobel Prize. Felix decided he was going to be the impetus for the planting of one billion trees in Germany and around the world. His stamina at such a tender age brought him worldwide media notice. He connected with like-minded people and groups in multiple countries and reached his goal by age eighteen.

Autumn Peltier discovered at age eight that her First Nations community on Manitoulin Island, within Lake Huron in Ontario, Canada, had contaminated drinking water. She turned herself into a "water warrior." In 2016, at age twelve, she publicly called out Prime Minister Justin Trudeau at the Assembly of First Nations for failing to protect her community's water. Her resolute environmental compass took her at age thirteen to speak during World Water Day at the United Nations General Assembly. Her address added intensity to the movement for this basic health right. The UN General Assembly and the Human Rights Council recognize access to safe drinking water as a human right.

Millions of people know that Greta Thunberg didn't wait. She is the Swedish youngster who at age nine was appalled that adults were ignoring the scientific evidence behind the worsening climate crisis. At age fifteen, every Friday she led school strikes in front of the Swedish Parliament. The media spread word of her determination to youngsters and adults around the world. The next year, she addressed the United Nations in New York—having *sailed* across the Atlantic because it's the most ecologically benign mode of transportation. She told the assemblage: "How dare you steal our future through inaction?"

Claire could have filled her book with many more such examples of youngsters who didn't wait. Sometimes the kids' inspiration came from their parents, sometimes from their teachers, such as Paula Rogovin, who got her kindergarten pupils interested in banning pesticides in New York City parks. She pursued this theme for the next seven years, joined by parents and health groups along the way. By 2021, on Earth Day, the New York City Council passed the ban, hearing the children over the pesticide lobby.

In another celebrated initiative, retired New York lawyer Robert Clampitt started, with his own money, the *Children's Express* to give kids between ten and thirteen highly visible opportunities to write and comment on important current affairs. They received credentials to attend the 1976 Democratic National Convention, where a thirteen-year-old, Gilbert Giles, broke the story that Jimmy Carter would pick Walter Mondale as his vice-presidential running mate.

Dr. Penny Owen instructed elementary and early high school students considered difficult to teach. Part of her lessons involved helping them to start a local cable television show in Winsted, Connecticut. The show dealt with serious local matters. She showed her students how to interview their grandparents and other relatives and turn their reporting into a story of their unique family histories. This connection with their family lineages helped anchor the students as they matured.

It is not surprising that the parents of these stand-up children were delighted with what their offspring were doing. The parents contributed to Penny's efforts by providing a supportive home atmosphere.

There are times when a child's pristine curiosity is the spark. One day, a fifth grader was walking to school in Salt Lake City, Utah, and she noticed "stuff" sticking out of a spare block of abandoned land. She eagerly told her teacher and classmates that she had discovered a waste dump nearby. Not possible, thought the teacher. The city would have done something or posted warning signs. To make a great story short, the little girl was right. The teacher organized them into an action project and got news coverage, leading the city to clean up the site. Later the students testified before the state legislature in support of a broader superfund law on waste dumps. So taken with what the students did, the teacher, Barbara Lewis, wrote a book in 1991 titled *The Kid's Guide to Social Action: How to Solve the Social Problems You Choose and Turn Creative Thinking into Positive Action* (Free Spirit Publishing) and delivered lectures around the country about how youngsters can civically engage, make change, and improve their classroom performance.

There are many opportunities for parents to enrich their children's formal education. A group of parents in Connecticut arranged an afternoon class for fifth graders on baking bread. The pupils learned about grain growing as well as dough preparation. Then a parent took them step by step through the baking processes and voilà, out came the loaves. The youngsters were proud of creating something real and delicious to take home to their parents and siblings. The parents were proud of their children and grateful for the gift of this experience.

Now compare this with what the giant, addictive industries of tobacco, alcohol, and opioids have done to youngsters through conscious, deliberate marketing to turn them into adolescent customers and victims. The tobacco industry also pushed addiction to nicotine until government and public opinion stopped the cigarette companies, which had been passing out free cigarettes in front of middle schools and high schools. "Hook them early and you've got them for life" was the marketing maxim in those dark decades before the tobacco companies were exposed and restrained. All kinds of illness and many premature deaths (over 400,000 a year) resulted from these marketers of death and addiction.

The alcohol industry was more subtle because of the visibility of drunkenness, especially associated with driving. They placed massive advertisements showing festive and healthy families holding beer cans or bottles. Then, as now, they placed ads urging "responsible drinking," and in the process get their full-page sales pitches in hundreds of college newspapers. About 150,000 people die each year in the US from alcohol-related diseases, with many more forms of family suffering, domestic violence, and fatalities on the highways related to alcohol abuse.

More recently, opioid manufacturers developed clever and deceptive promotions for relief of pain and other symptoms to sell tens of billions of dollars' worth of their pills, resulting in tens of thousands of overdose deaths each year in our country. The National Institute on Drug Abuse reports that "opioid-involved overdose deaths rose from 21,089 in 2010 to 47,600 in 2017 and remained steady through 2019. This was followed by a significant increase in 2020 with 68,630 reported deaths and again in 2021 with 80,411 reported overdose deaths."

Not a single executive of these three predatory industries—which were knowingly pushing dangerous substances in soothing language—was ever prosecuted and sent to prison. Had this happened, these big-time predators would be associating with felons languishing for years in penitentiaries for forging a few checks or other small swindles.

Corporate marketing madness would not have succeeded in its grisly missions were the schools educating the students openly and compellingly about these lethal products. Parents can fill these and other gaps in preparing their children to be healthier, upright, engaged citizens. We've heard several stories about informed children admonishing their mama and papa to stop smoking or to wear seat belts. Give young people accurate information and they will apply the knowledge. As my sister wrote: "If you have low expectations of children, they will oblige you; if you have high expectations, they will surprise you."

Our mother combined community service with the raising of four children. When asked how she could do both when the latter was clearly her priority, she replied, "What's the difference?" She meant that the two are tied together for the better, not the worse.

As an observant and active citizen, she noticed that many people didn't know much about their local community. At that time, Winsted had many factories, historical sites, natural tourist attractions, and all kinds of stores and farms sustaining a relatively self-reliant town. The town also had polluted waterways and air and some poverty. She attended to her civic duties and charitable activities. She also knew the importance of being a community educator. She once wrote a newspaper column titled "How to Tour Your Own Hometown" and gave copies to teachers.

Most communities teach very little about their own history, ecology, economy, and many other activities. She thought that was a major reason why generation after generation grows up without any sense of local civic duty beyond voting. People learn little about how all those offices in the town hall are supposed to work for the residents. It should be easy to get the schools to provide students with all sorts of local knowledge. There are almost always volunteer local historians or activists willing to lend a hand if there are no existing written materials available, as often is the case in small towns, villages, and rural areas.

Another area for school improvement is to reinstate physical education time, now abandoned by most schools to the detriment of students' health and improved classroom performance. The CDC reports, "Physical education provides cognitive content and instruction designed to develop motor skills, knowledge, and behaviors for physical activity and physical fitness."

Parental initiatives to greatly improve what children are given to eat in schools present realizable opportunities too serious to ignore. There is always a struggle between nutrition advocates and junk-food lobbyists over the Department of Agriculture's sharing of school lunch recipes. "The kids like our sugary, fat, and salty snacks," say these lobbyists. "You want them to eat what's on their dish, don't you?" The children exposed to thousands of ads became preconditioned to choose junk food over fresh fruit and vegetables or whole grain bread and cereals. Since 1980, the number of children with obesity, diabetes, and high blood pressure has risen sharply. Who better than informed parents, connected with impressive health-food groups and individuals, to turn the tide against these commercial exploiters of children's susceptibility to consume what is bad for them? The Center for Science in the Public Interest has a helpful website for parents looking for detailed suggestions on how to improve nutrition in schools. See: cspinet.org/protecting-our-health/healthy-school-lunches.

About forty years ago, some families in Indiana were aghast at what was sold in school vending machines. With a little study, they persuaded the school administrators to reserve space for nutritious items such as nuts and dried fruit. They managed to get national publicity for their efforts. Still, the candies persist in these machines and are chosen by the vendors instead of by the school nutritionist. Look into it.

About thirty-five years ago, I met the mother of one of our rising civic leaders. I inquired as to how he became such a star. She replied: "I spent a lot of time with him." She read books with him when he was a young child, took him to labor rallies, encouraged him to listen to adults discussing serious topics at their home, and included him in her and her husband's own civic and labor union pursuits.

Today, children are spending less time with adults—parents, relatives, neighbors—than at any time in human history. Their distance or separation has many causes: the omnipresent use of computers and so-called smartphones, the need for two-earner households, the decline of the proximate extended family, and the general emptying of sidewalks and front porches in favor of screen-watching. Moreover, the commercialization of childhood through direct marketing that bypasses parental guidance and control adds to this separation of children from their families.

Commercial intrusions upset my mother. Once, when the librarian at our Beardsley & Memorial Library was having difficulty getting young readers to return their borrowed books, the local McDonald's offered to give a free hamburger to youngsters who returned their overdue books. Mother thought that was wrong: the children should return the books on time because that was their responsibility, not because of some promotional incentive involving unhealthy food. She complained and she prevailed.

Her children noticed the power of the example set by both her and my father. To them, seeking a better, safer community was a natural part of living in a democracy. Whether we were watching my mother get US senator Prescott Bush to press the Army Corps of Engineers to build a dry dam to contain flooding, or witnessing my father's leadership during the aftermath of Hurricane Diana's wreckage of the town's businesses, or even watching them both speak at town meetings, my siblings and I absorbed their zest for taking self-government seriously.

It's about growing up civic and not growing up corporate. It's about avoiding the saturating impact of tens of thousands of TV, radio, and online advertisements. Advertisers promote a materialistic lifestyle. They have few reservations about selling often harmful goods and services. Logos and sly slogans bombard every nook and cranny of our children's worlds, including their clothing, schools, sporting events, and neighborhoods. The proliferation of rampant commercialism is more overwhelming online.

Building on an early civic life of participation with family and friends often leads to fuller activism and thought in high school and college. So many of the young civil rights leaders in the fifties and sixties, when asked, would attribute their start, their stamina, to their listening and watching their parents and the education they received at home. Indeed, my parents would tell us that we were receiving *training* (and some myths) at school, *inspiration* from our library, and *education* from our home.

There is no recipe for such civic upbringing. But there is some commonsense advice. Children can easily rebel; my parents instinctively understood this. They did not tell us to be active citizens. They taught indirectly, by their own example, and through short proverbial sayings ("You will lose your rights if you don't use your rights").

During my many campaigns and travels around the country and world, meeting with amazing champions of justice on behalf of all kinds of oppressed or deprived humans, I would pause to ask them how they came to be what they are—to have such drive, motivation, and purpose. Sometimes they would cite being part of a tragedy, a cruel act of force, greed, or exclusion. But quite often they would smile and respond with the following composite sentiment: well, in my youth, my parents, my mother, my father, my teacher, my neighbor, a relative told me, took me, showed me, inspired me. Scholars write many books about how a democracy can flourish; they do not often include regularly putting an arm around the shoulders of the young.

CHAPTER SEVEN

I, the Veteran

By now, our country should have very few veterans of lawful wars of defense. World War II, which ended in 1945, was the last war Congress declared under its exclusive constitutional authority to take us from a state of peace to a state of war. Instead, we have millions of veterans of wars undeclared by Congress but initiated by presidents on their unauthorized say-so. Congress has become comfortable with surrendering its constitutionally prescribed duties in this critical area to the overreaching White House. With little congressional supervision, presidents have used trillions of taxpayer dollars at the expense of our domestic needs, for destructive conflicts called "wars of choice."

As a result, the United States has drafted or induced millions of men and women into the armed forces to engage in wars and military "incursions" against countries that did not threaten, much less imminently imperil, our nation's safety. The driving force behind these invasions and the expansion of the American empire has been the political influence of large corporations and the complicity of military leaders. President Dwight D. Eisenhower (a five-star general in World War II), in his January 20, 1961, farewell speech, warned the nation about the "military-industrial complex," saying, "In the councils of government, we must guard against the acquisition of unwarranted influence, whether sought or unsought, by the military-industrial complex. The potential for the disastrous rise of misplaced power exists and will persist." He knew that arms industry's appetite for weapons of mass destruction and profits was insatiable.

Now the increasing automation of war-making, especially drone attacks carried out from comfortable computer chairs in Virginia and Nevada, is a foretaste of what's on the horizon that may come back to haunt our hitherto protected shores.

We continue to fund and staff a permanent Army, Navy, and Air Force. Military recruitment is enhanced by offering incentives to millions of Americans seeking to escape poverty, acquire an occupational skill, or save some money for education. Some find a career of twenty or thirty years appealing for the prospect of retirement benefits at a relatively younger age than when they might start receiving Social Security.

With few exceptions, veterans have learned to remain silent on their return home, or at least self-censor their real feelings about what they observed. They tolerate the politicians who flatter them and regale them with praise for "fighting to defend our freedoms." The horrors they witnessed, caused, and are afflicted by produce a moral and physical trauma that remains with them, often for years. Mental and physical pain suffered by veterans overwhelms efforts by families, physicians, and Veterans Affairs to treat the searing symptoms arising from the unleashed violence of massive mayhem.

The VA provides education benefits too, such as paying college tuition and offering career counseling. Military service can provide economic opportunities that may not be available to many and that serve as additional incentives to overstaff our armed services.

Veterans carry memories and insights that should be shared with civilians, the vast majority of whom neither know nor concern themselves with what their neighbors were doing abroad in their name. Civilians absolve their indifference with an occasional "Thank you for your service" greeting. More than a few returning veterans, coming from the many unnecessary wars against weak opponents who possess none of the massive weaponry of the US military, receive these thanks with an "I know better" nod. For, as many learned, invading the backyards of oppressed, impoverished people made military personnel hated as invaders. GIs are the quickest to realize that "we're not wanted there" and when back home silently question why we were there in the first place. In the field, however, as a soldier related, the common frustration came out with the repeated burst of "What the f*** are we doing here?" Millions of innocents, who were trapped in impoverished countries such as Korea, Vietnam, Laos, Cambodia, Afghanistan, Iraq, Libya, and many other regions of our tormented world, paid the price for US military adventures.

Under military law, soldiers are required to disobey clearly illegal orders. The International Military Tribunal at Nuremberg rejected "following Hitler's orders" defenses by senior Nazi officials who had committed war crimes, crimes against humanity, or wars of aggression. In Adolf Eichmann's trial in Jerusalem for, among other things, transporting Jews to death camps, the judges similarly denied that following orders was a defense. First Lieutenant William Calley's "following orders" defense was rejected in his My Lai massacre prosecution.

Presidential wars, i.e., wars not declared by Congress, such as the Korean War, the Vietnam War, the Iraq War, and the Libyan war, are clearly illegal and unconstitutional. Every participant in the drafting, debating, and ratifying of the Constitution applauded the Declare War Clause, which entrusts to Congress exclusive responsibility for breaking the peace in order to avoid the executive's propensity for gratuitous belligerency. This check serves to curb presidents from engaging in political exploitation, and jingoism. The US Supreme Court has never sustained the constitutionality of a presidential war, and it voiced doubts in *Youngstown Sheet & Tube Company v. Sawyer* (1952) (Korean War). Members of the US Armed Forces are thus obligated to disobey orders in furtherance of unconstitutional presidential wars.

Veterans enjoy full First Amendment rights to speak critically about wars not in self-defense, i.e., illegal wars of aggression. They are under no obligation to serve as a claque for the military after their service concludes.

A 2006 poll from Zogby International found that some three years after the illegal invasion pushed by President George W. Bush and Vice President Dick Cheney, 72 percent of US soldiers stationed in Iraq wanted the US to pull out within one year, and 25 percent wanted to leave immediately.

Leaving the armed forces does not erase the scars and brutal memories of the terrors of war—especially when those memories concern the deadly effects of war on families, as civilian fathers, mothers, and children turn out to be the primary victims. Veterans find they can only listen and recount to one another. At times, they gather in what they call "winter soldiers" meetings to exchange their dread, their nightmarish recollections, and their persistent mental and physical traumas. The media has shown little interest in their predicament beyond reporting veteran homelessness and suicides. The military brass and their supporters in Congress expect vets to remain mute, to shut up and hoist the flag of patriotism and demonstrate unquestioning loyalty to the armed conflicts, led so often by neoconservative legislators and officials who themselves found ways to avoid military service, from the time of the Vietnam War up to the dark term of Donald J. Trump. They and their successors are constantly hawking undeclared wars to be fought by others, not them. Fighting, killing, dying, or being permanently maimed is what Congress asks of others.

There are veterans who believe the flattery and join the American Legion or Veterans of Foreign Wars and accept the closed-minded mantra of "My country, right and wrong." But others choose to join smaller, unsubsidized groups, such as Veterans for Peace.

These veterans feel a calling to tell their stories and share lessons learned to the general population. They choose not to remain silent. They choose to convey the humanity of those millions of innocents abroad who have survived the massacres and remain stunned as to why the US attacked and left them in the debris of their communities or wandering as refugees searching for scraps of food and shelter. Some outraged vets work to rescue their interpreters or drivers left behind in Afghanistan and Iraq—the people who are unable to escape retribution at the hands of their countrymen after US soldiers pull out. Many veterans argue that those who worked with them should be brought to the US. The vets say their native comrades deserve more than the smoking rubble our war machine leaves behind.

Others push for special compensation for the many thousands of troops exposed to deadly toxic pollution from the burn pits operated by reckless corporate contractors to incinerate trash. In 2008, the *Military Times* reporter Kelly Kennedy published an article titled "Harmless or hazardous?" In 2022, the *Military Times* noted that "numerous studies and reports have suggested links between the poor air quality and rare cancers found in increasing numbers among post-9/11 veterans. The Department of Defense has estimated nearly 3.5 million troops from recent wars may have suffered enough exposure to the smoke to cause health problems."

Imagine contractors exposing our nation's fighting men and women to toxic fumes without adequate warning or protection. President Biden heard them and got Congress to enact a long-term appropriation of many billions of dollars for veterans filing disability claims. Taxpayers will pay, not the corporate contractors.

There is no end of causes for veterans that need to be pursued by the veterans themselves. There is the case of the devastating exposure in Vietnam of civilians and US soldiers to Agent Orange—a deadly defoliating chemical sprayed over thousands of square miles. Dow Chemical, Monsanto, and other companies that manufactured Agent Orange denied that the chemical harmed the vets. In a 1985 class action settlement, the companies agreed to establish a $180 million fund to finance a totally inadequate cash payment program for disabled veterans and survivors of deceased veterans. This war crime would have been submerged by the Pentagon and the contractors were it not for ailing veteran resisters finding the scientists and lawyers to help them. According to the United States Institute for Peace, "The Vietnam Red Cross estimates that three million Vietnamese have been affected by dioxin, including at least 150,000 children born after the war with serious birth defects." The US Agency for International Development has provided funds to assist people with disabilities in Vietnam, but nowhere near what is needed to help the people suffering because of the nineteen million gallons of Agent Orange sprayed on their country.

Too many vets have a hard time believing that they have extraordinary credibility when they speak about war being hell, or about the false propaganda behind the wars promoted by war hawks. Vets know many of our wars have nothing to do with protecting the US. Why is the US constantly messing around in other countries' backyards? Why haven't we learned that imperial European nations carving up various regions following World War I and the US dominating the globe after World War II have had disastrous consequences? Veterans, combining some history with their own experiences, can get people to listen who ordinarily would turn a deaf ear to civilian peace advocates. As one helicopter pilot told me, people should be interested in what veterans say about all the wasted billions of taxpayer dollars poured into busting up places overseas that could have been used to repair our country.

Veterans possess not only credibility but also knowledge about what was going on "over there" that the government keeps secret and the media doesn't or cannot satisfactorily expose, including about specific atrocities and war crimes. Sometimes vets need only be asked. A woman told me that once, while in a supermarket line, she struck up a conversation with a young soldier returning from Kabul. Curious, she asked, "What was your work over there?" He nonchalantly replied, that he unloaded cargo planes full of hundred-dollar bills for reshipment from Kabul airport to Kandahar (a provincial capital closer to hostilities). This threw light on the US government always exclaiming about corruption among the Afghans without mentioning who was a principal corrupter in those years. It also fortified the general story that the US military would bribe strategically located Taliban with hundred-dollar bills to let the US convoys pass through the mountains without being ambushed.

Veterans who break their silence can call out the lies and cover-ups that accompany all wars. As the saying goes, "In war, truth is the first casualty."

A veteran can go into the VA hospital or other medical clinics to treat their posttraumatic stress disorder. Much more difficult to treat is moral injury—which comes from killing innocents. Psychiatrist Jonathan Shay defines it as a "betrayal of what is morally right, by someone who holds legitimate authority, in a high-stakes situation." Moral injury and lethal danger and fear are inextricably tied to war. He gives the example of when a soldier goes to war to save the world from weapons of mass destruction, only to discover that they do not exist (in Iraq at least). As former representative Ron Paul said of Bush and Cheney, "They lied us into this war."

Some veterans find the only way to partially expiate this moral injury is to speak out against this war wherever and whenever they are given a chance.

Tomas Young was such a soldier. He joined the Army, believing the lies of Bush and Cheney, because of a patriotic calling. He also wanted to save some money for community college. While riding in a troop convoy after less than a week in Iraq, he was struck in the spine by a bullet, rendering him a paraplegic. He was transferred to Walter Reed Army Hospital in 2004. That was when his mother called me to say that, like her, Tomas was a reader, and they admired my works. She asked if I would visit him to lift his morale. I readily agreed and called the great TV talk show host Phil Donahue, who had recently been fired by MSNBC because he interviewed guests who opposed the Iraq War. Donahue said, "We were told we had to have two conservatives for every liberal on the show. I was considered a liberal. I could have Richard Perle on alone, but not Dennis Kucinich. You felt the tremendous fear corporate media had of being on the unpopular side during the ramp-up to war. And let's not forget that General Electric's biggest customer at the time was Donald Rumsfeld [then the Secretary of Defense]. Elite media features elite power. No other voices are heard." Donahue added, "And if you're General Electric, you certainly don't want an antiwar voice on a cable channel that you own."

I asked Phil to accompany me. We brought Tomas a bunch of books and spent nearly an hour with him and his mother. He spoke with some difficulty, as he was under pain medication.

Phil was so taken by this young soldier and what he was to face as he came to terms with his paralysis and his life in a wheelchair that he kept in touch, speaking with and counseling him regularly. He eventually produced a gripping documentary on Tomas called *Body of War*. The film recounted Tomas Young's evolution into an antiwar advocate and speaker who found purpose amid his daily pains, operations, and associated calamities.

There came a moment in 2014 when, despite being cared for by his loving wife, the pain and medical complications from his paraplegia became so unbearable that he lost his remaining will to live. His final act was to send a letter to the luxuriously retired president George W. Bush, who was receiving huge speech fees, book advances, and accolades from his adoring, hawkish audiences.

It was eleven and a half years after the Iraq War that, near death and in hospice, Tomas Young sent his "last letter" to George W. Bush and Dick Cheney. Here are some of his searing words:

I write this letter on behalf of husbands and wives who have lost spouses, on behalf of children who have lost a parent, on behalf of the fathers and mothers who have lost sons and daughters and on behalf of those who care for the many thousands of my fellow veterans who have brain injuries. . . . I write this letter on behalf of the some 1 million Iraqi dead and on behalf of the countless Iraqi wounded. I write this letter on behalf of us all—the human detritus your war has left behind, those who will spend their lives in unending pain and grief.

I write this letter, my last letter, to you, Mr. Bush and Mr. Cheney. I write not because I think you grasp the terrible human and moral consequences of your lies, manipulation and thirst for wealth and power. I write this letter because . . . I want to make it clear that I, and hundreds of thousands of my fellow veterans, along with millions of my fellow citizens, along with hundreds of millions more in Iraq and the Middle East, know fully who you are and what you have done. You may evade justice but in our eyes you are each guilty of egregious war crimes, of plunder and, finally, of murder, including the murder of thousands of young Americans—my fellow veterans—whose future you stole.

Your positions of authority, your millions of dollars of personal wealth, your public relations consultants, your privilege and your power cannot mask the hollowness of your character. You sent us to fight and die in Iraq after you, Mr. Cheney, dodged the draft in Vietnam, and you, Mr. Bush, went AWOL from your National Guard unit. Your cowardice and selfishness were established decades ago. . . . You sent hundreds of thousands of young men and women to be sacrificed in a senseless war with no more thought than it takes to put out the garbage.

I joined the Army two days after the 9/11 attacks.... I wanted to strike back at those who had killed some 3,000 of my fellow citizens. I did not join the Army to go to Iraq, a country that had no part in the September 2001 attacks and did not pose a threat to its neighbors, much less to the United States. I did not join the Army to "liberate" Iraqis or to shut down mythical weapons-of-mass-destruction facilities or to implant what you cynically called "democracy" in Baghdad and the Middle East.... I especially did not join the Army to carry out pre-emptive war. Pre-emptive war is illegal under international law. And as a soldier in Iraq I was, I now know, abetting your idiocy and your crimes. The Iraq War is the largest strategic blunder in US history.... I would not be writing this letter if I had been wounded fighting in Afghanistan against those forces that carried out the attacks of 9/11.... We were used. We were betrayed. And we have been abandoned. You, Mr. Bush, make much pretense of being a Christian. But isn't lying a sin? Isn't murder a sin? Aren't theft and selfish ambition sins? ...

My day of reckoning is upon me. Yours will come. I hope you will be put on trial. But mostly I hope, for your sakes, that you find the moral courage to face what you have done to me and to many, many others who deserved to live. I hope that before your time on earth ends, as mine is now ending, you will find the strength of character to stand before the American public and the world, and in particular the Iraqi people, and beg for forgiveness.

In the annals of military history, moral courage is much rarer than physical courage, in part because of the long-lasting sanctions against dissenters and those who speak truth to power about the faults in our own society. Tomas Young had both moral and physical courage. His example should be heeded by young soldiers in the future who are

ordered by gravely flawed politicians to make the ultimate
sacrifice for illegal follies and ambitions of our presidents
and their cronies.

Tomas Young's letter was sent to Bush in several ways to
ensure arrival, but it was never acknowledged by him or his tax-
payer-paid staff, nor accorded a respectful response. The lawless
president never looked back on the massive trails of blood and
destruction he caused. He was as immune to accountability as a
foreign dictator. Retired conservative judge Andrew Napolitano,
while he was a Fox News legal commentator, called for the Justice
Department to prosecute Bush and Cheney for gross war crimes.

After 9/11, a number of new veterans' groups emerged to stop
"endless wars" by mobilizing voters who were also veterans to
put pressure on legislators and the Pentagon. These are not the
organizations launched by the corporate Koch brothers and other
corporations for their own ideological profiteering or employment purposes. These are civic groups such as Veterans for Peace,
Iraq and Afghanistan Veterans of America, Common Defense,
Military Families Speak Out, and Iraq Veterans Against the War.
Their leaders traveled the country speaking out, forming chapters,
and distributing truthful information about what was going on
in those invaded countries. Some of their pleas made the major
media. Vietnam veteran Ron Kovic, who was shot in 1968 and
suffered a spinal cord injury that paralyzed him, wrote his best-
selling autobiography *Born on the Fourth of July*, which was made
into a popular Hollywood movie starring Tom Cruise. The dramatic film brought attention to our nation's lack of adequate
services for returning veterans who'd been badly wounded.

As the authors of the recent book *Our Veterans* note, "reform
efforts, led by Michigan congressman David Bonior and
others . . . [and the] resulting shake-up of the Department of
Veterans Affairs bureaucracy, which took several decades, ulti-

mately resulted in dramatic improvements in healthcare delivery, including making services more accessible via a network of community-based 'Vet Centers.'" None of this would have happened without the dramatic civic engagement of war veterans. This insightful book by Suzanne Gordon, Steve Early, and Jasper Craven does not sugarcoat the VA's paperwork delays nor the behavior of the Department of Defense and the weapons corporations. In its descriptions and disclosures, it gives veterans many road maps, connections, and openings for helping themselves, as well as encouraging them to wage peace, and dissolves the myths that hustle innocent young Americans into unnecessary wars and off to military bases in more than one hundred countries.

The 1974 book *The Discarded Army: Veterans After Vietnam*, by Paul Starr, with James Henry and Raymond Bonner, was an early warning about the plight of vets returning to our soil only to be left in the cold by the VA.

Other veterans have formed organizations that go to the crux of the country's self-devouring militarism, which is spurred by the endless profiteering appetites of the munitions companies such as Lockheed Martin, General Dynamics, Raytheon, and Boeing. In 1972, Rear Admiral Gene La Rocque and Rear Admiral Eugene Carroll, with other former high-ranking military leaders, started the Center for Defense Information. For some twenty years, it was a respected voice on the waste, redundancy, and corruption coursing through the out-of-control military budget. They knew about it from the inside. At one point, the CDI had a weekly program that aired on PBS stations all over the country. It also reached a significant audience in college classrooms and allied organizations via VHS distribution. The Center eventually merged into another Pentagon oversight group, as its founders had to confront Father Time. But they had set a sterling example.

Other retired high-ranking officers became formidable educators and advocates. After the CIA lied to secretary of state

Colin Powell about Saddam Hussein having weapons of mass destruction, Powell made his notorious speech at the United Nations, justifying the invasion of Iraq, which he later described as "a blot" on his career. Powell's then chief of staff, retired colonel Larry Wilkerson, was so outraged that, after retirement, he became one of the nation's blazing truth-tellers. Teaching at William & Mary and writing, lecturing, and networking with other retired officers around the country, he continues to be a sane, sagacious force for analytic accuracy in the fundamental pursuit of peace and justice.

In interviews and letters to their families, some veterans have poured their hearts and souls and their cogent and factual observations into writings that were then largely ignored by the corporate media. An exception was Erik Edstrom—a West Point graduate and Afghanistan war veteran who opened his eyes, rejected myths, and began to think clearly about how to reach his fellow soldiers and shake Americans free of their indifference. The result was his 2020 page-turner of a book, *Un-American: A Soldier's Reckoning of Our Longest War*. He takes the reader from a fascinating critique of West Point's mind-shaping to the raw realities of America's undeclared wars of choice, which are replete with ongoing lies and manipulations of public opinion. He describes these wars not only as tragedies but also as crimes, adding that "perhaps the greatest tragedy is that society lacks the conviction to say those who prosecuted these wars are criminals. If a millennium of the dead could speak: There is no betrayal more intimate than being sent to kill or die for nothing, by your own countrymen."

If you as a veteran are hesitant to speak out and heed Edstrom's honest pleas for you to hold these armchair politicians accountable or fire them, there is page after page that will fortify your sense of right and wrong and provide you with compelling facts, insights, judgments. He says, "If the public wants to think more than thank, it needs to end the legislative madness: reassert

Congress' war powers, clip the Pentagon's brass parachutes and rationalize the military budget."

When entering the civic arena—and on your journey to help people become more assertive in waging peace and stopping preventable wars that could go nuclear—one of the better outlets is the aforementioned Veterans for Peace (which has chapters nationwide). I am a member. See veteransforpeace.org. Its members are veterans of wars ranging from World War II all the way to the present war-making era. They are earnest and effective. You'll see how firmly they are grounded in broad principles and indisputable facts. You'll scan the range of positions they have democratically adopted. You can see their record of demonstrations and lobbying based on a broad context of social justice. Study their website. Those who attend annual Veterans for Peace conventions immediately find the solidarity they have sought. They are not alone. They work with other peace groups to increase their impact (the whole is greater than the sum of its parts). With headquarters in the heart of the country—St. Louis, Missouri—they are looking to increase their frugal budget to support full-time watchdogs over Congress in Washington, D.C. Congress needs such determined organizations to stop its blank checks for the bloated military budget that too often funds the savagery of empire, resulting in harm and deprivations being inflicted on the American people and wanton destruction of countries and their inhabitants abroad.

From the foregoing remarks, I hope you can see various points of entry from your present situation. Keep in mind, the easiest initial outreach is to share your observation of the immense waste and contractor rip-offs with your friends and neighbors. Specific examples, as in the case of contractors charging the Pentagon for $450 claw hammers, enrage the public. One general observed that a widely publicized example—the staggering price for a toilet seat cover—did more to outrage people than detailed reports of billions of dollars wasted by the same weapons corporations.

Early in the attack on Iraq, contractors sold contaminated drinking water to soldiers. The Wall Street Journal reported that "in July 2003 alone, a Saudi subcontractor hired by KBR billed for 42,042 meals a day but served only 14,053 meals a day. The difference for that month was more than $3.5 million." Marie deYoung, a former army chaplain who worked for Halliburton, said KBR, a Halliburton subsidiary, charged soldiers $45 for a case of soda and $100 to wash 15-pound bag of laundry. The short but enraging documentary *Iraq for Sale: The War Profiteers* (tagline: "Who's getting killed. Who's making a killing.") will generate indignation from all viewers, regardless of their political beliefs.

Having opened your neighbors' minds to the facts, you can move to challenge the abuses of runaway big-business interests that propelled empire, damaging our country while increasing hatred of Americans by the devastated peoples overseas (some of whom seek revenge for the loss of their loved ones). Your fellow veterans and citizens will be amenable to the truth and common sense that you are conveying. It gives meaning to what you have experienced and endured as a soldier and helps answer that grief-ridden question: for what? Lest we forget our innocent mass victims, veterans can remember publicly, for example, the anniversary of the brutal sociocide of the Iraqi people—March 19–20, 2003.

Postdischarge life in America is difficult for many reasons. One of them is that the vast public is clueless about these wars beyond the overwhelming propaganda and lies used to justify them. This governmental and corporate manufacturing of support or indifference is not a good climate to help with your pain, anguish, or economic circumstances.

A nonmedical, twelve-step model of veterans helping veterans could be inexpensive for the country. Many professionals are not comfortable treating veteran problems so extensively with medicines that often either do not work, have adverse side effects, or both. A nonmedical model could advance human interaction between veterans at local centers to which vets can come daily and engage in a variety of educational, civic, and recreational activities with minimum health and safety supervision. For more information, see: maketheconnection.net/read-stories/veterans-group-therapy.

Veterans can also benefit from what has worked for their buddies in other areas, which could be adopted as a best practice by other localities or communities. All these suggestions are driven by the avoidable plague of loneliness that affects so many returning soldiers—a loneliness that, as you know, can lead to psychological and physical traumas, sometimes resulting in debilitating homelessness or suicide.

The voices of veterans, who have the credibility of lived experience and are exposed to risks or actual injuries, can become the voices of a muscular peace, replacing the boomeranging explosions of criminal wars of empire leading to ever bigger collisions from which the US mainland may no longer be spared. Remember, despite the blitz of phony, manipulative patriotism, when the truth reaches the people, peace will out-poll war by overwhelming margins.

CHAPTER EIGHT

I, the Philanthropist

People who seriously strive for justice often recoil when it is suggested that to have necessary human and material resources for systemic changes and redirections, reasonable attempts should be made to seek assistance from some of the very wealthy. "Don't you understand that *they* are the problem?" is the retort from some advocates for a more just society. This stereotype closes off their creativity and doesn't address the history of philanthropy for justice.

But not all very rich people (VRP) are the same. Some are not the problem and have proved this. There are enough examples of determined mavericks in our past to motivate these current VRP to extend such a legacy into the future.

Whatever their motivations—guilt, empathy, search for a life purpose, memorializing their loved ones, ingratiating themselves with their admonishing children, or reacting to a terrible event—wealthy Americans have helped bankroll the American Revolution, the early drive to abolish slavery, the women's suffrage movement, the plight of unorganized workers, and, more recently, the civil rights, antiwar, environmental, consumer, and women's struggles for justice. Even some public-interest law firms and prisoners' rights initiatives have been launched with VRP money.

At the local level, charitable donations are often used to build or sustain important community institutions, but giving rarely goes beyond gifts to traditional charities.

In my hometown of Winsted, Connecticut, William L. Gilbert, the wealthy owner of the Gilbert Clock Company, built the first high school, and another wealthy person established the first library in memory of her husband. In addition, two Winsted philanthropists established the first hospital in our county.

Of course, VRP have endowed foundations to donate to universities, colleges, libraries, and religious orders. Their donations are viewed by challengers of the status quo as bandages at best or as co-optations of potential resistance at worst. Philanthropy, however, is not always that simple.

Other VRP have funded institutions of justice. The former CEO of Midas Muffler, Gordon Sherman, established Business and Professional People for the Public Interest, a formidable nonprofit public-interest law firm that took on the Chicago establishment, from banks to polluters. Another justice-geared philanthropist has been the major funder of *Democracy Now!*, a radio and TV program based in New York City, which is anchored by the persistent progressive Amy Goodman. A group of business-people organized Business Executives Move for Vietnam Peace which, during the Vietnam War, became a key force working to finally end that devastating debacle in 1975.

Rich steel magnate Andrew Carnegie underwrote library-building projects in towns across the US and Canada, so long as the communities provided the land as an expression of their steadfast commitment to this endeavor. Many a serious fighter against injustice got their start reading in one of the more than 1,600 of those libraries in America alone.

Carnegie—who had a history of forcefully cracking down on rebellious, striking workers, had something of an epiphany late in his life. He wrote the classic book *The Gospel of Wealth*, in which he concluded, "The man who dies thus rich dies disgraced."

With this background, let's start with the role assumed by more than two hundred very rich people in the United States who signed on to the Giving Pledge, conceived by Warren Buffett and Bill Gates. Each person pledged to "give the majority of their wealth to philanthropy either during their lifetimes or in their wills." The idea emerged from the friendship between these avid bridge players. Buffett, who had his own family foundation, would often say there aren't many good new ideas in philanthropy appealing to people who know how to make a lot of money but don't have a clue as to what to do with it, including him. Over the years, trusting Bill Gates and his then-wife, Melinda, and marveling at the success of Microsoft, whose technology he confessed not to understand, Buffett decided on the largest philanthropic commitment in American history. He pledged to give about $30 billion to the Gates Foundation over ten years, or about $3 billion a year. The Gates Foundation works on global public health and US educational projects and has 1,400 employees. That immense gift was an example of actions speaking louder than words as Buffett started calling other VRP to join in the Giving Pledge.

This effort paradoxically hamstrung itself because a condition of membership was not to lobby one another on behalf of this or that program. Pledge-takers would decide for themselves how much and where to donate. That may have been necessary to attract pledgers, but it also worked to dampen the likelihood of funding for new, bold, systemic justice ideas or other controversial projects. Traditional charities are often the default recipients of donations from cautious or indifferent donors. The pledgers meet twice a year and have made just one exception for an invited person to attend and make a pitch. That was the late Dr. Paul Farmer, the celebrated hands-on builder of health clinics in remote, impoverished areas of Haiti and West Africa.

The absence of transformative ideas, à la Buffett's observation, is not due to a lack of awareness of the omnicidal trends plaguing the fragile planet or the preventable poverty, suffering, and repression that characterize many societies, including our own. The knowledge of grave, root abuses of humanity and the perilous risks rapidly emerging from modern concentrated control of capital and technology are quite visible to the VRP. What drains their imagination ab initio? How can they elevate their own sense of significance? Their lack of experience in breaking new ground or enabling civic achievements that reduce inequities often stems from settling on important but safe charitable activities.

How can you, the VRP, strengthen America as a deliberative democratic society, one substantial and courageous enough to earn the undying respect of posterity (a word often used by our country's founders)?

Let's start with any condition or privilege that already angers you. Choose one where you have regularly complained to people at dinners or other gatherings. It just tees you off. So you are predisposed to seek a remedy. Why don't you take the next steps? Define your goal, develop a strategy for action, determine how much civic investment it would take, and launch your effort.

Let's say you're a businessperson who has always been accountable to shareholders, and you are steamed about the waste, fraud, and abuse in the gigantic, unaudited Pentagon budget. You know the Chief Financial Officers Act was enacted in 1990. This simple law requires federal agencies to conduct annual audits. Congress passed this legislation because, as the text of the act says, "Billions of dollars are lost each year through fraud, waste, abuse, and mismanagement among the hundreds of programs in the Federal Government." In April 2023, Representative Barbara Lee (D-CA) and others introduced the Audit the Pentagon Act of 2023 because as of November 2022, the Pentagon has been unable or unwilling to complete an audit of its sprawling spending around the world. Representative Lee said, "The lack of accountability and transparency at the Pentagon is simply outrageous. Congress pours trillions of taxpayer dollars into the Pentagon, but we still have no clear idea how that money is being spent." Her bill will reduce the Pentagon budget by a small percentage each year if it fails to produce an audit.

This is really shameful, you think, as does every certified personal accountant in the US. Probably 99 percent of the American people polled would agree. Further supermajorities would dislike the findings by the congressional Government Accountability Office that show chronic waste of billions of taxpayer dollars. Senator William Proxmire (D-WI) presented "Golden Fleece" awards to federal agencies that initiated or allowed wasteful, gigantic cost overruns or fraud by corporate contractors. Without audited inventories, the Air Force, for example, has spent huge sums on supplies and spare parts that they now cannot locate at more than a hundred bases throughout the world. The general public should demand an end to the redundancy of each service wanting its own special weapon systems, often with harmful results to soldiers. There are many traditional weapons of mass destruction, such as aircraft carriers or unneeded planes with limited functions. In the era of modern precision missiles, and now armed drones, carriers are as vulnerable as sitting ducks.

The more you probe, the more you become interested in who is doing something about it. Not Congress. They hardly hold hearings. Unfortunately, the Republicans and the Democrats are on the same "Give the Department of Defense more than it asks for" page regarding the endless wars of aggression. A few groups, such as Project On Government Oversight, the Quincy Institute, and Veterans for Peace, have demonstrated and written in opposition to the Moloch-like bloated budget. The big veteran associations, such as the American Legion and Veterans of Foreign Wars, support burgeoning military budgets and wars. A small number of citizen groups, with their tiny budgets, struggle to monitor and check the overreaching Pentagon.

Ergo: the vacuum is ready for your "plunge." You know what must be started. First, publicize the facts more widely, including statements by every secretary of defense since the 1990s pledging to produce an auditable budget in five years or less. It has not happened. It is time to strengthen the staff capabilities of existing civic and veterans' groups and assemble serious citizen units, with expertise, at the state level. It is also important to elevate the legislators who can be the champions on Capitol Hill on a day-to-day basis to become members of the House and Senate armed services committees and to join the ranks of the leadership in Congress. You'll be surprised at how many people from many backgrounds, along with veterans, will join you once they see your leadership and know they can count on your resources.

This is a problem with a solution. The missing ingredient is financial support for citizen organizing.

Maybe you're in the brokerage business and can't tolerate influential venture capitalists who avoid billions of dollars a year in taxes and get their carried-interest commissions wrongly treated as lower capital gains taxes rather than as ordinary income, which is taxed at much higher rates. Or maybe you've made your wealth in lifesaving technologies, and you are incensed by the wasteful, corrupt, price-gouging health insurance system, which causes many people to go without the health care they need (about 100,000 Americans a year die as a result). Instead, you want health insurance for all Americans—think "Medicare for all." Or maybe what really worries you is the impending climate catastrophe and a gridlocked Congress that is not mitigating or preventing it.

You start asking: "Isn't anyone in my upper economic class doing anything about these avoidable messes, so long tolerated by Congress?" You find out, to your dismay, that the answer is, astonishingly, no. You become intrigued. From your business experience, you understand that if you make no investment in a good idea, it remains just that—an idea in some entrepreneur's head. By the same token, with investment in a bad idea or policy, lawmakers predisposed to campaign cash are likely to give the superrich what they want.

With just a little research reading books such as Daniel Callahan's *The Givers: Wealth, Power, and Philanthropy in a New Gilded Age* (2017), you'll see that those big philanthropists and their foundations are giving to just about every sector you can imagine. They give large amounts to research in education, health, medical, and other scientific pursuits. Their giving helps to alleviate poverty, promote population control, finance children's programs, avert climate crises, facilitate more efficient government, proselytize for free-market ideology, advocate for lower taxes and reduced regulation, underwrite libraries, sponsor think tanks, and take on tobacco and street drugs. These funders give to every cause you could think of, right down to detailed projects in specific cities, election administration, the arts, abortion, human rights, even to projects aimed at closing coal plants or diminishing overfishing. You name it, they are funding it on one side or another—or both.

There are even grants by the heirs of wealthy ancestors directly opposed to the source of their inherited wealth. Descendants of Texas oil barons and the Rockefellers are pushing for conversion from fossil fuels to solar and other renewable energies. Some of these grants have achieved considerable success, as with support for understanding the causes and remedies of autism or asthma. Others have served only to intensify the existing powers and controls over our country and world on the part of their class. Often, the result is, in Callahan's words, that "through their giving, they are wielding even more influence. . . . Giving . . . can be yet another tool to advance partisan goals and class interests. In effect, it can be a way of taking."

Some of these big givers have fattened the purses of right-wing think tanks, such as Heritage and Cato, to push successfully for tax cuts for very wealthy individuals and large corporations. Some are big campaign funders for politicians reducing taxes on contributor's fortunes and income. Lobbyists for the super-rich and corporations have successfully pushed the federal government to establish the lowest tax rates and biggest loopholes in modern times.

Then there are the many causes they promote which on their face are humanitarian advances yet so often don't go the last mile and therefore fail their declared missions. These disconnects are mostly not accidental; the givers' charitable intentions don't have the stamina to override either their class interests or the controversy or retaliation that may come from going all the way.

For example, many of these donors wish to improve education, and they have chosen to do so by funding private charter schools rather than improving public education. These hundreds of charter schools have not fulfilled donor predictions and often do the harm of taking the least needy pupils out of the public schools. Donors want to teach these students about free enterprise, but not the civic skills and experiences that will tie together in a motivated and equitable way the various subjects the students are expected to master.

Other donors support children's well-being, but they do not lobby Congress for paid family sick leave, paid daycare, or a livable wage for parents. Even modest pressure on their GOP friends in Congress would have led to an extension in 2022 of the child tax credit that had cut our disgraceful child poverty by one-third.

Some megadonors push for more science and technological know-how, but other than demanding from Congress more subsidies for companies and grants to universities, their know-how somehow did not lead them to demand reauthorization of the crucial Congressional Office of Technology Assessment, defunded by former Speaker Newt Gingrich in 1995. Supported by virtually the entire world of science and technology, OTA was advising Congress on how to avoid technological and scientific boondoggles costing many billions of dollars as well as how to regulate emerging technologies.

Many donors pursue better health outcomes by funding hospitals, medical schools, and clinics, but they can't get themselves to press for universal health insurance and health care. Many other Western countries have that, helping them head off or minimize massive, preventable human casualties—death, injury, sickness, expenses, family anguish, and the horrendous toll on patients and workers that our present corrupt, gouging, exclusionary system imposes.

Large donors may give here and there to alleviate the impending climate crisis or to encourage renewable energy policies. But their focused lobbying on Capitol Hill is almost nil. The pro and con votes on important energy issues haven't moved since 2009–2010, when an attempt was made, in vain, to enact a House-passed comprehensive national energy conversion, blocked by a threatened filibuster in the Senate.

Other donors fund many drives to reduce the national deficit but are AWOL when the GOP and sometimes the Democratic Party cut huge revenues that would have come from the very rich and large corporations. Some 60 percent of major corporations pay no federal income tax on their US-based profits; others pay at far lower rates than the official cap of 21 percent. It is not difficult to discern which priorities are supreme here.

Over a decade ago, some very rich people stopped talking and started lobbying Congress for tax increases on the rich, including themselves: the Patriotic Millionaires (although they are multi-millionaires). These businesspeople mean business, and they have about twenty full-time staff in Washington who go in and out of congressional offices making the case with determination and tough written materials, including their most recent book, *Tax the Rich! How Lies, Loopholes, and Lobbyists Make the Rich Even Richer*. They also know how to generate media coverage of their advocacy.

Read their mission statement:

> We believe that the trend of growing economic inequality is both bad for society and bad for business. We believe revenue models that rely on human misery should be exorcised from our economy. We believe the government should mandate a livable wage for all working Americans, rather than relying on "the market" which has failed to realize that goal over 240 years of American history. We believe a national "living wage" law will ensure a stable level of aggregate demand, which will fuel our economy

more broadly, ushering in a new era of prosperity for all Americans, including rich ones.

We believe our nation's social and economic progress requires significant and constant public investment, and that the wealthy, who benefit the most from our country's assets and institutions, should naturally and gladly pay the greatest share of whatever taxes are needed to support that investment.

Most Americans, regardless of political party, support this philosophical framework. Political power currently lies primarily with those who don't. The task ahead is difficult but relatively straightforward. We must grow the political power of those committed to this framework, and diminish the political power of those who are not committed to this framework.

Every American deserves as much political power as millionaires;

Every American who works full time should be able to afford their basic needs;

Millionaires and large corporations—who have benefited most from our country's assets—should pay a larger percentage of the tab for running the country.

They specify with concrete numbers what the tax rate should be and target the loopholes that should be eliminated. Because they have ongoing involvements in the business world, they know the tricks of avoidance and evasion tax lawyers are using. That's one reason they are supporting a long-overdue budget increase for the GOP-depleted Internal Revenue Service. The Patriotic Millionaires understand that the IRS has to recruit very skilled corporate tax specialists to pursue the giant tax escapes and hundreds of billions of dollars that go uncollected each year. They nonetheless keep pressing for a breakthrough.

What this all leads to is my urging that you assemble a wide variety of projects, causes, and networks suitable to your temperament, knowledge, values, and locale and then see which of them will prompt you to put the suitable forces in motion in whole or in part.

Then make a plan. You can start with this question: what is the key institution powerful enough to either block or enact legislation dealing with major redirections and reforms supported by the majority of our country? The obvious answer is Congress. Yet over and over again, the "good guy" donors continue to ignore this powerful institution and instead keep hitting stone walls back home regarding their chosen philanthropic mission. Aside from protecting their own vested interest, these "good guys" are either lacking in tactical or strategic imagination or prejudging the possibility of failure in what they see as a gridlocked or dysfunctional Congress or state legislature. They don't see that the majority of the 535 members of Congress are able to be persuaded by a tiny fraction of people back home who know what they are talking about, who reflect majority opinion—even supermajority opinion—and stay focused on the decisional forum that can bring success. Thinking wholesale does not displace thinking retail in politics. Grassroots organizing and education—the retail side of politics—is a prerequisite in producing lasting, fundamental change.

Let's say you discover that the people *own* the greatest wealth in our country but do not *control* what they own. *Control* is in the hands of corporations through their influence over our government, which is the trustee for our expansive commons. The commons includes the vast onshore and offshore public lands, the public airwaves, and the extensive taxpayer funds for research and development that have launched or grown most of the major industries in our nation and provided intellectual property used to create pharmaceutical products and even the internet, which was based on the Defense Department's creation of Arpanet. You wonder why these takeovers are not political issues for public deliberation before and after elections. You add up the trillions of dollars commonly owned in the form of mutual funds and pension funds invested in stocks and bonds that are controlled by corporate managers and brokers. Restoring control in sensible ways to the people—the owners—and their intermediaries would improve livelihoods and protect these assets for future generations. It would increase the educational awareness that property is not just what individuals, families, and corporations own—it's what we all own together. Restoring control to the owners would poll very well, to say the least.

You get excited and do some research at bollier.org—that is David Bollier's website about the commons and how to "think like a commoner." (See *Think Like a Commoner: A Short Introduction to the Life of the Commons*, one of his several books on the subject.) You read and get steamed at how control of the commons is turned against the very owners, from gouging fees by brokers to the leaving of environmental damage to taxpayers, to the giveaway at ridiculous prices of public lands such as forests and mines. You are incredulous when you read that the General Mining Act of 1872, unamended since, allows any US or foreign corporation that discovers "hardrock" minerals—such as gold, silver, or molybdenum—on public lands to lease or seek title to that land from the federal government for no more than $5 per acre. You are aghast when you read that a Canadian gold-mining company—Barrick Gold Corporation—"purchased" 1,038 acres for $5,190, or $5 per acre. Barrick got $10 billion worth of gold in Nevada, and Uncle Sam got robbed. Taken all together, you wonder whether this is the biggest ongoing giveaway in American history. Your piqued curiosity leads to the discovery that the primary lobbyists fighting to protect public lands are the environmental groups led by Earth Works and outdoor recreation companies led by Patagonia. News reports say Patagonia's first-ever television advocacy campaign ad, which cost the company $700,000, urged customers and environmentalists to stand up against the Trump administration and defend America's public lands. Patagonia also sued during the Trump administration to halt taking the public lands private.

You conclude that there is not enough opposition to the shrinking of public lands, and even less civic or commercial pressure to make companies pay for their use or extractions at fair market prices. But what really astounds you is the vacuum confronting the giveaway of the public airwaves. Zero enforcement of the Federal Communications Commission rule that requires broadcast station owners to provide the public with programming that meets the federal standard described as "the public interest, convenience and necessity." You stopped watching TV years ago and are disgusted by the degradation of the content on our airwaves. Even worse, trillions of dollars in government research and development are just given away to private corporations. Waste and abuse characterize the massive corporate contracts with the government. You check and find there is little congressional oversight on anything that can be called "the commons." On Capitol Hill, the message of inaction or complicity is, "Do whatever you want with the public's resources, assets, and revenue. Just keep your campaign cash coming our way." You start getting angry, and you have the money to do something about it. You launch a $2 million mass media campaign announcing the formation of Commons Preservation Associations (CPAs) in as many congressional districts as meet your criteria. That means a minimum critical number of joiners, volunteer hours, and dues.

The purpose: public awareness and watchdogging Congress, district by district. Links to and advice from informed people and groups will start flowing. You are underway and have found your labor of love, which has led to meaning for the ages, daily excitement and challenges, wonderful colleagues, and more love from your grandkids.

Still want more choices? Review Harvard University professor Malcolm Sparrow's findings on billing fraud in the health care industry—at least a billion dollars a day. An applied mathematician, Sparrow wrote the groundbreaking book *License to Steal* in 1997 (updated in 2000). He has testified before public bodies, but the health care industry has lobbied government officials to maintain the corrupt status quo. He explains that the minimum enforcement budget to handle such huge looting should be 1 percent. That would mean $3.5 billion a year. In fact, that is about what the federal government recovers on a tiny enforcement budget within the Department of Health and Human Services. Once again we see that the massive vacuum created by an underfunded citizen drive has massive consequences.

Congress has been ignoring this theft since before its Government Accountability Office estimated in 1992 that 10 percent of health care expenditures are lost through fraud, ghost billing, and padded billing. Over $60 billion a year is taken from the Medicare budget alone. The rule of law here is MIA. Oversight of the insurance industry at the federal and state level is a farce.

Enter a VRP like you. You know the drill and the details. Reducing corporate waste, fraud, and abuse requires bigger strategic enforcement budgets, more prosecutions, and mass media coverage to make curtailing corruption a political campaign issue. Isn't it time for some law and order for commercial crimes? Watch the great support you'll get from the people who obviously end up paying for corporate abuses and weak government oversight. The total amount saved by ending fraud would provide health insurance coverage for almost all uninsured and underinsured Americans.

Maybe you are more taken with the sterling opportunity to save lives from "preventable problems" in US hospitals. A peer-reviewed study from the Johns Hopkins School of Medicine in 2015 conservatively estimated that five thousand preventable deaths per week occurred in hospitals alone, not counting casualties connected to clinics and physician offices.

One would think that this and other previous studies would have galvanized one or more of the medical associations to put their best foot forward and get moving on reform. Members of the American Medical Association are in every hospital in the country. They know. "Preventable problems include medical malpractice, hospital-induced infections, understaffing, harmful prescription drug combinations, mishaps in moving or responding to patients, misdiagnosing and more." All these fall within the responsibility of a profession dedicated to the principle "do no harm." You are properly shocked when you see how little these medical societies have done, how few hospital administrations have taken seriously this avoidable epidemic of their own making, and how easily some actual progress has occurred, such as getting doctors, nurses, and nursing assistants to thoroughly wash their hands between patients.

Following the Johns Hopkins report, the media devoted a short article to these astounding conclusions. No one in Congress picked up the cudgels. Nor did state legislatures, state public health departments, or the hospital accreditation organizations. The only action came from the small consumer groups specializing in health care. Part of the reason for this lassitude is the lack of any grassroots mobilizations, which is usually required to jolt policymakers to move on a problem. Groups operate on what they think is feasible, and if they think nothing is going to happen even if they try, they are prepared for failure, not success. That's where you can come in and network the incipient forces into motion, one state department of health or public health association—or one senator or representative or governor or attorney general—at a time. This is a movement waiting to happen. We know what needs to be done. Once reform efforts have wheels, activists will get rolling.

Let's say you want to start with a more personal connection.

Say you love trees. You have beautiful oaks, maples, rare elms, and chestnut trees on the land surrounding your home. Recently you've been reading about the remarkable, intelligent life of trees and how they sustain themselves and respond to external pressures as they age. Your love of trees has gotten you outside more and away from the screens that absorb so much of your work and recreational time. You yearn for your children or grandchildren to break out of their internet incarceration and connect with nature too. You realize that many children have little access to nature, especially in cities and paved-over suburbs. Some do, though, because their community has an arboretum. Aha—a bulb goes on in your head. Why not help establish arboretums all over our country? Do what Carnegie did for libraries. Announce that if the community supplies the land—anywhere from two acres or more—then your arbor experts will visit these communities with their expertise and help the public officials and citizen groups make the most of this land by planting biological varieties—trees, bushes, and other plants. As a magnet for school trips, adult education, or just local tourism, it is hard to find a better way to connect with and understand the wonders of nature and the contribution of trees to the world's climate health. Daily addictions to a digital world of virtual reality, social media, and AI algorithms are separating people, especially youngsters, from their families, communities, nature, and the self-consciousness critical to a maturing mind grappling with the realities of life. You'll find tree enthusiasts flocking to participate in their pursuit of "Every town an arboretum."

Let's assume that you are into getting youngsters to fill a large gap in their formal education by learning to be skilled citizens—so essential to a functioning, productive democracy. With your wealth, you can initiate after-school clubs to develop civic skills and civic experience in the community. There are lots of hands-on civic advocates who will see such a venture as manna from heaven, for the young are our future, and the planet is running out of time.

Harvard professor Robert Coles has written several insightful books, replete with interviews, showing that even young children have a refined sense of right and wrong—a moral intuition that too many adults have lost to opportunity costs.

There are resources on the horizon to connect youngsters with so many great civic organizations. They see your determination, which, as my mother used to advise, "puts their dreams on wheels." There has been much thinking about how safely supervised civic engagement can help maturing young people. Some innovative models have been advanced by the Kettering Foundation, under the leadership of by David Matthews, which has provided a wealth of information on ways the citizenry can strengthen our democracy. This institution, produces publications, such as the magazine *Connections*, and insightful reports on civic engagement. Sharon Davies, new the president and CEO of Kettering, will be implementing the organization's updated strategic plan that makes countering authoritarianism a top priority for Kettering.

Children, when informed of society's injustices and remedies, can display a marvelous moral authority directed toward adults, starting with their own families. Informed children admonishing their parents to wear their seat belts or to stop smoking in years past have shaken father and mother into "wanting to be there" for their children and grandchildren. The ultracommercialization of childhood, with major corporations directly marketing to children and bypassing parental authority and guidance, has further deepened the need for elders to protect these children from such punishing pressures that induce them to nag their parents and demand products harmful to their physical and mental health.

As previously described, corporate marketing madness would not have succeeded in its grisly missions were the schools educating the students openly and compellingly about these lethal products. Parents can fill these and other gaps to prepare their children to be healthier, more engaged citizens. Give young people accurate information and they'll figure out how to apply the knowledge.

After-school clubs can interact with each other across the land for joint projects or to spread best practices to spark the curiosity, imagination, and intellect of practical young idealists. You can get this launched and adopted in many communities. The National Conference of State Legislatures notes that regular participation in after-school programs "has been linked to lower dropout rates and a narrowing of achievement gaps, particularly among low-income students." Youngsters and their parents would welcome such programs.

By now, I hope I have conveyed that the projects desirable for people of great wealth to transform society's ills into assets are limitless. To show what I have long believed, I placed a full-page announcement in the *Baltimore Sun*, on October 4, 2014, proposing "a new American tradition: birth-year gifts to America." It contained twenty-five initiatives of importance to all the people in our country.

Explaining further, I wrote: "Americans born in each of the same birth years can together fund their own legacy gift to lift our country's future. For example, the birth years of 1928, 1929, 1930, 1931, 1932, 1933, 1934, and so on." It is a major expansion of university alumni classes whose graduates in the same year make a gift to their alma mater. I continued: "Together people in each birth year can advance significant, self-renewing nonprofit civic institutions to improve the life prospects of our descendants starting now." Below are some national and local examples to stimulate your imagination and ideas about what your gifts could accomplish:

Herewith the list:

1. Organizing after-school clubs for civic skills and civic experience in the community;
2. Establishing a national Showing Up for Citizen Engagement Day to rediscover a better America;
3. Advancing affordable open access to justice forums for all Americans (including using small-claims courts);
4. Making it easier to create more self-reliant communities;
5. Awarding moral-courage awards in all 3,007 counties in America to encourage and support people who stand tall;
6. Preserving and enhancing the valuable commons owned by the people, for the people;
7. Creating facilities for participatory neighborhood sports—both organized and unorganized;
8. Advancing nutritious, delicious food consumption for all ages;
9. Enacting public financing of public elections, and other electoral reforms to give voters more choices and voices;
10. Organizing veterans—the men and women who have experienced preventable violence—against war;
11. Accelerating the end of dire poverty and hunger in a wealthy world;
12. Advancing civic participation in politics to produce the benefits of a democratic society;
13. Organizing congressional accountability watchdog groups in all congressional districts;
14. Organizing the enlightened superrich against war and poverty, and for progressive tax reform;
15. Organizing scientists and technologists to consider the consequences of their work directly and by others;

16. Promoting ways for faster conversion to solar energy and energy efficiency;

17. Providing adequate enforcement budgets for corporate violations;

18. Instituting broad prison reform and rehabilitation, for adults and juveniles;

19. Advancing full "Medicare for all," greater efficiency in health care, and free choice of doctors and hospitals;

20. Ending most taxpayer bailouts;

21. Fostering a lean, efficient defense and advancing an international arms-control movement and conflict resolution without violence;

22. Building 2,000 community civic centers, as Mr. Andrew Carnegie did when he built over 1,600 free libraries in the US;

23. Endowing departments of civic practice in universities and colleges so students can learn how to practice democracy, civil rights, and civil liberties;

24. Activating the older generations of Americans to share their wisdom and experience with the young; and

25. Creating arboretums in communities nationwide.

birthyearlegacy.org

Neither the project in this relatively small urban newspaper nor the distribution of reprints drew much of a serious response. No editorials or columnists picked up the birth-year approach. The whole concept of a birth-year tradition, with its examples, needs a VRP promoter. It is permissible to hope that this volume will reach VRP to stimulate their individual or collective civic deliberation, for present and future generations.

Conclusion

Now that you have reviewed the eight roles for a strong democracy, it may occur to you that moving yourself further along these pathways is nowhere near as difficult as the challenges you have overcome in life. For example, raising children, overcoming a family tragedy or serious illness, and staying afloat financially are much harder than extending yourself into the various citizen roles presented in this book.

It is simply more pleasurable to live life when you have developed more power by exercising your civic muscle. There is less agony, anguish, and frustration when you are not feeling disempowered. You also don't get ripped off as much. You're likely to attract like-minded allies in your neighborhood, workplace, and marketplace. You will view elections as a time to voice your concerns and enlist others in the fight to make candidates for office responsive to the people rather than the corporations.

For too many people, daily life can be repetitious, tedious, and downright distressing. Growing into these eight roles makes your daily routines less humdrum and creates something more to look forward to each day, if only because you are interacting with many people in a myriad of supportive ways.

As I have noted, my father used to say, "If we don't use our rights, over time we will lose our rights." You will discover how to use those rights, which most people don't use and don't even know about. This will empower you. Few consumers or workers use the small-claims courts that are everywhere in our country and are easy to use. Wrongfully injured workers and consumers rarely use the law of torts with a contingency-fee attorney to secure their constitutional right to trial by jury. In some states, such as California, consumer laws give you the right to sue companies that engage in unfair, deceptive, or misleading practices. The Internal Revenue Service has a Taxpayer Advocate Service, which has proven helpful in connecting people with IRS experts or to answer questions about IRS services. People underuse the freedom of information laws at the state and federal level. Citizens can request government information such as food inspection reports, reports on defective products, and many other documents produced by our public servants.

The Federal Trade Commission has excellent advisory pamphlets on almost every major product or service—all free. A whole world of possibility opens up when you start looking for these little-used opportunities—many of which were brought into being by the pressure of early citizen activists over the decades.

You will enjoy other gratifications as well. If you are one of the several million people who learned CPR from the local EMT or medical institution, you are ready for emergencies you might encounter—at a supermarket, a public meeting, or a sports event. The same is true for refining your practice of democracy to use in different civic emergencies. One never knows when these enhanced skills may be needed—you might use them in the case of a workplace calamity, a harm inflicted on many consumers, a political scandal, a problem at the local school, or the drumbeat for a preventable war.

Do you know who has that kind of "be prepared" attitude besides the Boy Scouts? Anyone who learned how to fix simple plumbing, electrical, or carpentry problems that can suddenly arise in your home knows the value of being prepared. Same for learning a little about fixing your simpler computer problems.

Then there are the headlines we would like to ignore but can't because they are about looming perils that are not ignoring us. The rise of sea levels is already threatening millions of residents in cities such as Houston, Galveston, New Orleans, Miami, and New York City. The abrupt emergence of ChatGPT-type advances is raising novel questions and risks once considered to be the stuff of science fiction. Out-of-control autonomous robots will reduce the number of apathetic bystanders. The technological threats to human existence, beyond atomic weapons, are increasing. Just think of one dimension: autonomous weapons directing themselves, which are already in advanced development.

As more people enhance their roles in democracy, more varied talents, temperaments, and diverse bases of knowledge will fortify us in our fight against the erosion of our rights. And the example you and your colleagues will set is of an elevated public citizen practiced, experienced, and prepared to improve our society.

As you engage in this way of life, you can become a role model for the younger generations, who you can enlist to follow in your footsteps. Even elementary school children will seek to follow your example in civic projects in the places they are being raised. New community events—such as Earth Day, Food Day, and, in Canada, Citizen's Day—can become traditions. All the roles for a strong democracy are consistent with America's best historic traditions and values. All will help reduce the painful experiences associated with poverty, preventable diseases, and other traumas afflicting our country at present.

Redressing the stark imbalances of power afflicting workers, consumers, and veterans leads to imagining and achieving new realities. Political exclusion and economic exploitation are inconsistent with a true democracy. There is no reason for us to fear or exaggerate the obstacles and problems before us once we as a society choose to be prepared to foresee and forestall them, for "We the People," being smarter and more capable collectively than any one individual, can overpower our problems with adaptive solutions.

We'll end where we began: by reiterating that civic self-respect leads to a functional civic personality; that we must acquire knowledge within the context of justice and connect what we know to civic action.

Remember, it doesn't take more than 1 percent of adult citizens—citizens who know what they are talking about and reflect the value of fair play shared by a majority of the citizenry—to focus decisive civic energy on the designated decision-makers in our legislatures and other forums. One percent is all we need to successfully address public need and make the changes necessary for us to live in a good society. That is the fundamental lesson to be learned from the best of our ancestors and forebears. We should carry with us the immortal words of ancient Rome's greatest lawyer, Marcus Tullius Cicero: "Freedom is participation in power." And as Mahatma Gandhi said, "Be the change you wish to see in the world."

Appendix

The Citizen's Summons to a Member of the Congress

Whereas, the Congress has tolerated the expansion of an electoral process, corrupted by money, that nullifies our votes and commercializes both congressional elections and subsequent legislation, creating a Congress that is chronically for sale;

Whereas, the Congress has repeatedly supported or opposed legislation and diverted the taxpayer dollars to favor the crassest of corporate interests to the serious detriment of the American people, their necessities, and their public facilities—such as access to safer consumer products, health care, and other basic social safety services. It has opposed raising the inflation-ravaged minimum wage and fair taxation, allowed endemic waste, fraud, and abuse by contractors, and authorized massive corporate welfare subsidies and giveaways;

Whereas, the Congress has narrowed or blocked access to justice by millions of Americans, leaving them unprotected and defenseless in many serious ways, while giving business corporations preferential treatments and allowing them full access to influence the three branches of government;

Whereas, the Congress has imposed trade treaty despotisms over our democratic institutions—the courts, legislatures, and executive departments and agencies—subordinating our domestic branches of government's abilities to preserve and enhance labor, consumer, and environmental standards to the domination of global commerce's "bottom line" and endorsed the usurpation of our judicial process by secret tribunals under the WTO, and other similar invasions of US sovereignty;

Whereas, the access to members of Congress has increased for corporate lobbyists and decreased for ordinary citizens, Therefore, the citizens of the [INSERT state (for Senators) or the congressional district (for Representatives)] hereby summon you to a town meeting(s) during the August recess at a place of known public convenience. Your constituents will establish an agenda of how Congress should shift long-overdue power from the few to the many, both in substantive policy and through the strengthening of government and civic institutions;

We deem this Summons to be taken with the utmost seriousness as we gain grassroots support throughout your congressional district (or state for Senators). We expect to hear from you expeditiously so that the necessary planning for our town meeting can take place. This Peoples' Town Meeting reflects the Preamble to the Constitution that starts with "We the People" and the supremacy of the sovereignty of the people over elected representatives and corporate entities;

Be advised that this Summons calls for your attendance at a Town Meeting run by, of, and for the People. Please reserve a minimum of two hours for this serious exercise of deliberative democracy.

Sincerely yours,

The names of citizens and citizen groups

Resources for Action

Reading

CHAPTER 1. I, THE CITIZEN

Bonner, Robert J. *Aspects of Athenian Democracy*. Berkeley: University of California Press, 1933.

Bowen, Catherine Drinker. *Miracle at Philadelphia: The Story of the Constitutional Convention*. Boston: Little, Brown and Company, 1966.

Chambers, Edward T., and Michael A. Cowan. *Roots for Radicals: Organizing for Power, Action, and Justice*. New York: Continuum, 2003.

Frank, Joshua. *Atomic Days: The Untold Story of the Most Toxic Place in America*. Chicago: Haymarket Books, 2022.

Garland, Anne Witte. *Women Activists: Challenging the Abuse of Power*. New York: The Feminist Press, 1988.

Gibbs, Lois. *Achieving the Impossible: Stories of Courage, Caring, and Community*. Falls Church, Va.: Center for Health, Environment, and Justice, 2008.

———. *Love Canal: My Story*. Albany: State University of New York Press, 1982.

Greider, William. *Who Will Tell the People: The Betrayal of American Democracy*. New York: Simon & Schuster, 1992.

Hightower, Jim. *Thieves in High Places: They've Stolen Our Country—and It's Time to Take it Back*. New York: Viking, 2003.

Hunn, Dwayne L., and Doris Ober. *Ordinary People Doing the Extraordinary: The Story of Ed and Joyce Koupal and the Initiative Process*. Los Angeles: People's Lobby, 2001.

Isaac, Katherine. *Civics for Democracy: A Journey for Teachers and Students*. Washington, D.C.: Essential Books, 1992.

Isaacson, Walter S. *Benjamin Franklin: An American Life*. New York: Simon & Schuster, 2003.

Lerner, Barron H. *One for the Road: Drunk Driving since 1900.* Baltimore: Johns Hopkins University Press, 2011.

Nader, Ralph. *Breaking Through Power: It's Easier Than We Think.* San Francisco: City Lights Books, 2016.

———. *The Seventeen Solutions: Bold Ideas for Our American Future.* New York: Harper, 2012.

———. *The Good Fight: Declare Your Independence and Close the Democracy Gap.* New York: Regan Books, 2004.

———. "Democratic Revolution in an Age of Autocracy." *Boston Review* 18, no. 2 (1993): 8-10, 12.

———. "Toward an Initiatory Democracy." In *Action for a Change: A Student's Manual for Public Interest Organizing,* by Ralph Nader and Donald K. Ross, pp. 3-14. New York: Grossman Publishers, 1972.

Nader, Ralph, and Carl J. Mayer. "Corporations Are Not Persons." *New York Times,* April 9, 1988, 31.

Rakove, Jack N. *Original Meanings: Politics and Ideas in the Making of the Constitution.* New York: Alfred A. Knopf, 1996.

Smith, Sam. *Sam Smith's Great American Political Repair Manual.* New York: W. W. Norton & Company, 1997.

CHAPTER 2. I, THE WORKER

Boyer, Richard O., and Herbert M. Morais. *Labor's Untold Story.* 3rd ed. New York: United Electrical, Radio, and Machine Workers of America, 1976.

Clifford, Steven A. *The CEO Pay Machine: How It Trashes America and How to Stop It.* New York: Blue Rider Press, 2017.

Ehrenreich, Barbara. *Nickel and Dimed: On (Not) Getting By in America.* New York: Metropolitan Books, 2001.

Freeman, Richard B., and Joel Rogers. *What Workers Want.* Ithaca: Cornell University Press, 1999.

Geoghegan, Thomas H. *Which Side Are You On? Trying to Be for Labor When It's Flat on its Back.* New York: Farrar, Straus, and Giroux, 1991.

Greider, William. *The Soul of Capitalism: Opening Paths to a Moral Economy.* New York: Simon & Schuster, 2003.

Lasson, Kenneth L. *The Workers: Portraits of Nine American Jobholders.* New York: Grossman Publishers, 1971.

Levy, Karen. *Data Driven: Truckers, Technology, and the New Workplace Surveillance.* Princeton, N.J.: Princeton University Press, 2022

Nader, Ralph. *Getting Steamed to Overcome Corporatism: Build It Together to Win.* Monroe, Me.: Common Courage Press, 2011.

Nader, Ralph, Peter J. Petkas, and Kate Blackwell. *Whistle-Blowing.* New York: Grossman Publishers, 1972.

Page, Joseph A., and Mary-Win O'Brien. *Bitter Wages.* New York: Grossman Publishers, 1973.

Shaw, Christopher W. *Undermining Safety: A Report on Coal Mine Safety.* Washington, D.C.: Center for Study of Responsive Law, 2008.

Taft, Philip. *Organized Labor in American History.* New York: Harper & Row, Publishers, 1964.

Teixeira, Ruy, and Joel Rogers. *America's Forgotten Majority: Why the White Working Class Still Matters.* New York: Basic Books, 2001.

Wilson, William Julius. *When Work Disappears: The World of the New Urban Poor.* New York: Vintage Books, 1997.

CHAPTER 3. I, THE CONSUMER-SHOPPER

Brock, James W., ed. *The Structure of American Industry.* 13th ed. Long Grove, Ill.: Waveland Press, 2016.

Green, Mark J., and Nancy Youman. *The Consumer Bible: 1,001 Ways to Shop Smart.* Rev. ed. New York: Workman, 1998.

Green, Mark J., with Kevin McCarthy and Lauren Strayer. *Defend Yourself! How to Protect Your Health, Your Money, and Your Rights in Ten Key Areas of Your Life.* New York: Newmarket Press, 2006.

Johnston, David Cay. *Fine Print: How Big Companies Use "Plain English" to Rob You Blind.* New York: Portfolio/Penguin, 2012.

Nader, Ralph. *The Frugal Shopper Checklist Book: What You Need to Know to Win in the Marketplace.* Washington, D.C.: Center for Study of Responsive Law, 1995.

———. "The Consumer Movement Looks Ahead." In *Beyond Reagan: Alternatives for the '80s,* edited by Aaron Gardner, Colin Greer, and Frank Riesman, pp. 271-85. New York: Harper & Row, 1984.

———. "The Great American Gyp." *New York Review of Books* 11, no. 9 (1968): 27-34.

———. "The Safe Car You Can't Buy." *Nation* 188, no. 15 (1959): 310-13.

Nader, Ralph, and Wesley J. Smith. *Winning the Insurance Game: The Complete Consumer's Guide to Saving Money.* Rev. ed. New York: Doubleday, 1993.

———. *The Frugal Shopper.* Washington, D.C.: Center for Study of Responsive Law, 1992.

Radin, Margaret Jane. *Boilerplate: The Fine Print, Vanishing Rights, and the Rule of Law.* Princeton, N.J.: Princeton University Press, 2017.

Rosenfield, Harvey. *Silent Violence, Silent Death: The Hidden Epidemic of Medical Malpractice.* Washington, D.C.: Essential Books, 1994.

Sullivan, Bob. *Gotcha Capitalism.* New York: Ballantine Books, 2007.

Tellado, Marta. *Buyer Aware: Harnessing Our Consumer Power for a Safe, Fair, and Transparent Marketplace.* New York: Public Affairs, 2022.

Whittelsey, Frances Cerra, and Marcia Carroll. *Women Pay More: And How to Put a Stop to it.* New York: New Press, 1995.

Wolfe, Sidney M. *Worst Pills, Best Pills: A Consumer's Guide to Avoiding Drug-Induced Death or Illness.* New York: Pocket Books, 2005.

CHAPTER 4. I, THE TAXPAYER

Barlett, Donald L., and James B. Steele. *The Great American Tax Dodge: How Spiraling Fraud and Avoidance Are Killing Fairness, Destroying the Income Tax, and Costing You.* Boston: Little, Brown and Company, 2000.

———. *America: Who Really Pays the Taxes?.* New York: Simon & Schuster, 1994.

Bollier, David. *Silent Theft: The Private Plunder of Our Common Wealth.* New York: Routledge, 2002.

Johnston, David Cay. *Free Lunch: How the Wealthiest Americans Enrich Themselves at Government Expense (and Stick You with the Bill).* New York: Portfolio, 2007.

———. *Perfectly Legal: The Covert Campaign to Rig Our Tax System to Benefit the Super Rich—and Cheat Everybody Else.* New York: Portfolio, 2003.

Lewis, Charles, and Bill Allison. *The Cheating of America: How Tax Avoidance and Evasion by the Super Rich Are Costing the Country Billions.* New York: William Morrow, 2001.

Morgensen, Gretchen, and Joshua Rosner. *These Are the Plunderers: How Private Equity Runs—and Wrecks—America.* New York: Simon & Schuster, 2023.

Murphy, Richard J. *Dirty Secrets: How Tax Havens Destroy the Economy.* London: Verso, 2017.

Nader, Ralph. *Cutting Corporate Welfare.* New York: Seven Stories Press, 2000.

———. "It's Time to End Corporate Welfare as We Know it." *Earth Island Journal* 11, no. 4 (1996): 36-37.

———. "No More Bailouts!" *Mother Jones* 15, no. 6 (1990): 22-23.

———. "Remarks before the Conference on Property Tax Reform (1970)." In *The Ralph Nader Reader*, by Ralph Nader, pp. 233-41. New York: Seven Stories Press, 2000.

Rowe, Jonathan. *Our Common Wealth: The Hidden Economy That Makes Everything Else Work.* San Francisco: Berrett-Koehler Publishers, 2013.

Saez, Emanuel, and Gabriel Zucman. *The Triumph of Injustice: How the Rich Dodge Taxes and How to Make Them Pay.* New York: W. W. Norton & Company, 2019.

Sears, David O., and Jack Citrin. *Tax Revolt: Something for Nothing in California.* Cambridge, Mass.: Harvard University Press, 1982.

Zucman, Gabriel. *The Hidden Wealth of Nations: The Scourge of Tax Havens.* Translated by Teresa Lavender Fagan. Chicago: University of Chicago Press, 2015.

CHAPTER 5. I, THE VOTER

Dionne, E. J., and Miles S. Rapoport. *100% Voting: The Case for Universal Voting.* New York: New Press, 2022.

Farah, George F. *No Debate: How the Republican and Democratic Parties Secretly Control the Presidential Debates.* New York: Seven Stories Press, 2004.

Green, Mark J. *Selling Out: How Big Business and Corporate Money Buys Elections, Rams Through Legislation, and Betrays Our Democracy.* New York: Regan Books, 2002.

Hill, Steven J. *Fixing Elections: The Failure of America's Winner Take All Politics.* New York: Routledge, 2002.

Lewis, Charles. *The Buying of the President.* New York: Avon Book, 1996.

Nader, Ralph. *Crashing the Party: Taking on the Corporate Government in an Age of Surrender.* New York: Thomas Dunne Books, 2002.

———. "The Concord Principles: An Agenda for a New Initiatory Democracy." In *The Ralph Nader Reader,* by Ralph Nader, pp. 40-46. New York: Seven Stories Press, 2000.

———. "Breaking Out of the Two-Party Rut." *Nation* 255, no. 3 (1992): 98-101.

———. "Must Candidates Avoid Free T.V.?" *New York Times,* October 8, 1984, A19.

Piven, Frances Fox, and Richard A. Cloward. *Why Americans Don't Vote.* New York: Pantheon Books, 1988.

Reynolds, David B. *Democracy Unbound: Progressive Challenges to the Two Party System.* Boston: South End Press, 1997.

Richie, Robert, and Steven J. Hill. *Reflecting All of Us: The Case for Proportional Representation.* Boston: Beacon Press, 1999.

Rosenstone, Steven J., Roy L. Behr, and Edward H. Lazarus. *Third Parties in America: Citizen Response to Major Party Failure.* 2nd ed. Princeton, N.J.: Princeton University Press, 1996.

Stern, Philip M. *Still the Best Congress Money Can Buy.* Washington, D.C.: Regnery Publishing, 1992.

———. *The Best Money Congress Can Buy.* New York: Pantheon Books, 1988.

CHAPTER 6. I, THE PARENT

Boyles, Deron R. *American Education and Corporations: The Free Market Goes to School*. New York: Garland Publishing, 1998.

Buschman, John E. *Libraries, Classrooms, and the Interests of Democracy: Marking the Limits of Neoliberalism*. Lanham, Md.: Scarecrow Press, 2012.

Harty, Sheila. *Hucksters in the Classroom: A Review of Industry Propaganda in Schools*. Washington, D.C.: Center for Study of Responsive Law, 1979.

Hewlett, Sylvia Ann, and Cornel R. West. *The War Against Parents: What We Can Do for America's Beleaguered Moms and Dads*. Boston: Houghton Mifflin Company, 1998.

Jacobson, Michael F., and Laurie Ann Mazur. *Marketing Madness: A Survival Guide for a Consumer Society*. Boulder, Colo.: Westview Press, 1995.

Lewis, Barbara. *The Kid's Guide to Social Action: How to Solve the Social Problems You Choose—and Turn Creative Thinking into Positive Action*. Minneapolis: Free Spirit Publishing, 1998.

Linn, Susan. *Who's Raising the Kids? Big Tech, Big Business, and the Lives of Children*. New York: New Press, 2022.

———. *Consuming Kids: Protecting Our Children from the Onslaught of Marketing and Advertising*. New York: New Press, 2004.

Molnar, Alex, and Faith Boninger. *Sold Out: How Marketing in School Threatens Children's Well-Being and Undermines Their Education*. Lanham, Md.: Rowan & Littlefield, 2015.

Nader, Claire. *You Are Your Own Best Teacher! Sparking the Curiosity, Imagination, and Intellect of Tweens*. Washington, D.C.: Essential Books, 2022.

Nader, Ralph. "Children: Toward Their Civic Skills and Civic Involvement." *Social Education* 56, no. 4 (1992): 212-14.

Nader, Ralph, and Linda Coco. *Children First! A Parent's Guide to Fighting Corporate Predators*. Washington, D.C.: Corporate Accountability Research Group, 1996.

Schor, Juliet. *Born to Buy: The Commercialized Child and the New Consumer Culture*. New York: Scribner, 2004.

Taylor, Betsy. *What Kids Really Want That Money Can't Buy: Tips for Parenting in a Commercial World*. New York: Warner Books, 2004.

CHAPTER 7. I, THE VETERAN

Bacevich, Andrew J., and Daniel A. Sjusen, eds. *Paths of Dissent: Soldiers Speak Out Against America's Misguided Wars*. New York: Metropolitan Books, 2022.

Black, George. *The Long Reckoning: A Story of War, Peace, and Redemption in Vietnam*. New York: Alfred A. Knopf, 2023.

Edstrom, Erik N. *Un-American: A Soldier's Reckoning of Our Longest War*. New York: Bloomsbury Publishing, 2020.

Ehrhart, W. D. *Marking Time*. New York: Avon Books, 1986.

Gonzalez, Roberto J. *War Virtually: The Quest to Automate Conflict, Militarize Data, and Predict the Future*. Berkeley: University of California Press, 2022.

Gordon, Suzanne, Steve Early, and Jasper Craven. *Our Veterans: Winners, Losers, Friends, and Enemies on the New Terrain of Veterans Affairs*. Durham, N.C.: Duke University Press, 2022.

Greider, William. *Fortress America: The American Military and the Consequences of Peace*. New York: Public Affairs, 1998.

Harris, David V. *Our War: What We Did in Vietnam and What it Did to Us*. New York: Times Books, 1996.

Hartung, William D. *Prophets of War: Lockheed Martin and the Making of the Military-Industrial Complex*. New York: Nation Books, 2011.

Hedges, Chris. *The Greatest Evil Is War*. New York: Seven Stories Press, 2022.

Jamail, Dahr. *The Will to Resist: Soldiers Who Refuse to Fight in Iraq and Afghanistan*. Chicago: Haymarket Books, 2009.

Koistinen, Paul A. C. *State of War: The Political Economy of American Warfare, 1945–2011*. Lawrence: University Press of Kansas, 2012.

Sheehan, Cindy. *Dear President Bush*. San Francisco: City Lights Books, 2006.

Starr, Paul E., James F. Henry, and Raymond P. Bonner. *The Discarded Army: Veterans After Vietnam*.New York: Charterhouse, 1973.

Van Devanter, Lynda, with Christopher Morgan. *Home before Morning: The Story of an Army Nurse in Vietnam*. New York: Beaufort Books, 1983.

CHAPTER 8. I, THE PHILANTHROPIST

Bollier, David. *Think Like a Commoner: A Short Introduction to the Life of the Commons*. Gabriola Island, Canada: New Society Publishers, 2014.

Callahan, David. *The Givers: Wealth, Power, and Philanthropy in a New Gilded Age*. New York: Alfred A. Knopf, 2017.

Collins, Chuck, Pam Rogers, and Joan P. Garner. *Robin Hood Was Right: A Guide to Giving Your Money for Social Change*. New York: W. W. Norton & Company, 2000.

Curti, Merle, Judith Green, and Roderick F. Nash. "Anatomy of Giving Millionaires in the Late 19th Century." *American Quarterly* 15, no. 3 (1963): 416-35.

Dowie, Mark C. *American Foundations: An Investigative History*. Cambridge, Mass.: MIT Press, 2001.

Farmer, Paul E. *Partner to the Poor: A Paul Farmer Reader*. Berkeley: University of California Press, 2010.

Foster, Lawrence G. *Robert Wood Johnson: The Gentleman Rebel*. State College, Pa.: Lillian Press, 1999.

Krass, Peter. *Carnegie*. New York: John Wiley & Sons, Inc., 2002.

Lagemann, Ellen Condliffe. *The Politics of Knowledge: The Carnegie Corporation, Philanthropy, and Public Policy*. Middletown, Conn.: Wesleyan University Press, 1989.

Nevins, Allan, and Frank Ernest Hill. *Ford: Decline and Rebirth, 1933-1962*. New York: Charles Scribner's Sons, 1962.

Pearl, Morris B., and Erica Payne. *Tax the Rich! How Lies, Loopholes, and Lobbyists Make the Rich Even Richer*. New York: New Press, 2021.

Philpott, Gordon M. *Daring Venture: The Life Story of William H. Danforth*. New York: Random House, 1960.

Price, Robert E. *Sol Price: Retail Revolutionary and Social Innovator*. San Diego: San Diego History Center, 2012.

Rapoport, Bernard, with Don E. Carleton. *Being Rapoport: Capitalist with a Conscience*. Austin: University of Texas Press, 2002.

Sparrow, Malcolm K. *License to Steal: How Fraud Bleeds America's Health Care System*. 2nd ed.Boulder, Colo.: Westview Press, 2000.

Groups

CHAPTER 1. I, THE CITIZEN

Ballot Access News, https://ballot-access.org/
Center for Health, Environment, and Justice, https://chej.org/
Industrial Areas Foundation, https://www.industrialareasfoundation.org/
Mothers Against Drunk Driving, https://madd.org/
NAACP, https://naacp.org/
The People's Lobby, https://www.thepeopleslobbyusa.org/
Physicians for a National Health Program, https://pnhp.org/

CHAPTER 2. I, THE WORKER

Capitol Hill Citizen, https://www.capitolhillcitizen.com/
National Employment Lawyers Association, https://www.nela.org/

CHAPTER 3. I, THE CONSUMER-SHOPPER

Better Business Bureau [criticized], https://www.bbb.org/

Better World Club, https://www.betterworldclub.net/
Center for Science in the Public Interest, https://www.cspinet.org/
Consumer Reports, https://www.consumerreports.org/
Flyers' Rights, https://flyersrights.org/
National Cooperative Bank, https://www.ncb.coop/
Public Citizen, https://www.citizen.org/

CHAPTER 4. I, THE TAXPAYER

Center for Responsive Politics (now called Open Secrets), https://www.opensecrets.org/
Citizens for Tax Justice, https://ctj.org/
Good Jobs First, https://goodjobsfirst.org/
The Patriotic Millionaires, https://patrioticmillionaires.org/
Taxpayers for Common Sense, https://www.taxpayer.net/

CHAPTER 5. I, THE VOTER

The Hightower Lowdown, https://jimhightower.substack.com/
Houston Property Rights Association, (No Webpage)
Poor People's Campaign, https://www.poorpeoplescampaign.org/

CHAPTER 6. I, THE PARENT

*Center for Science in the Public Interest, https://www.cspinet.org/

CHAPTER 7. I, THE VETERAN

Common Defense, https://www.commondefense.us/
Iraq and Afghanistan Veterans of America, https://iava.org/
Iraq Veterans Against the War, https://www.ivaw.org/ (Inactive since 2017)
Military Families Speak Out, https://militaryfamiliesspeakout.com/
United States Institute for Peace, https://www.usip.org/
Veterans for Peace, https://www.veteransforpeace.org/

CHAPTER 8. I, THE PHILANTHROPIST

Business and Professional People for the Public Interest, https://www.macfound.
    org/grantee/business-and-professional-people-for-the-public-interest-444/
The Gates Foundation [Should this really be included? No], https://www.gates-
    foundation.org/
The Patriotic Millionaires, https://patrioticmillionaires.org/
Partners in Health, https://www.pih.org/
Project on Government Oversight, https://www.pogo.org/
Quincy Institute, https://quincyinst.org/